Hugo's Simplified System

John + Norm Smith

Spanish
Phrase Book

D1306931

Hugo's Language Books Limited

Compiled by
Lexus Ltd
with
Alicia de Benito de Harland
and
Mike Harland

Facts and figures given in this book were correct when printed. If you discover any changes, please write to us.

5th impression 1990

Set in 9/9 Plantin Light by
Typesetters Ltd and
printed in England by
Courier International Ltd, Tiptree, Essex

CONTENTS

CONTENTS

PREFACE

This is the latest in a long line of Hugo Phrase Books and is of excellent pedigree, having been compiled by experts to meet the general needs of tourists and business travellers. Arranged under the usual headings of 'Hotels', 'Motoring' and so forth, the ample selection of useful words and phrases is supported by an 1800-line mini-dictionary. By cross-reference to this, scores of additional phrases may be formed. There is also an extensive menu guide listing approximately 600 dishes or methods of cooking and presentation.

The pronunciation of words and phrases in the main text is imitated in English sound syllables, and highlighted sections illustrate some of the replies you may be given and the signs or instructions you may see and hear.

PRONUNCIATION

When reading the imitated pronunciation, stress that part which is underlined. Pronounce each syllable as if it formed part of an English word, and you will be understood sufficiently well. Remember the points below, and your pronunciation will be even closer to the correct Spanish. Use our audio cassette of selected extracts from this book, and you should be word-perfect!

H: represents the guttural sound of 'ch' as in the Scottish 'loch'. *Don't* pronounce this as lock.

I: (small capital letter) rhymes with 'eye'

s: always sound the Spanish 's' as a double 'ss' as in 'missing', *never* like 's' in 'easy'.

th: as in 'thin', *not* as in 'they'.

Don't be worried by the varying pronunciations you are certain to hear in some parts of Spain, for example the sounding of 'z' (and of 'c' before e or i) like an English 's' ... although in this instance we'd recommend that you *don't* copy it, but lisp the sound as we have imitated it. Similarly, in certain circumstances, the Spanish 'v' can be pronounced as either a 'v' of a 'b' so that 'vaca' sounds like 'baca' - as you'll hear in our recording.

USEFUL EVERYDAY PHRASES

Yes/No
Sí/No
see/noh

Thank you
Gracias
grath-yass

Please
Por favor
por fa-vor

I don't understand
No comprendo
noh komprendoh

Do you speak English/French/German?
¿Habla usted inglés/francés/alemán?
ah-bla oosteh eengless/franthess/alleh-man

I can't speak Spanish
No hablo español
noh ah-bloh esspan-yoll

Please speak more slowly
Por favor, hable más despacio
por fa-vor, ah-bleh mass desspath-yoh

Please write it down for me
Por favor, escríbamelo
por fa-vor, esskreeba-meh-loh

Good morning/good afternoon/good night
Buenos días/buenas tardes/buenas noches
bweh-noss dee-ass/bweh-nass tardess/bweh-nass notchess

Hello
Hola
oh-la

Goodbye
Adiós
ad-yoss

How are you?
¿Cómo está usted?
koh-moh essta oosteh

Excuse me please
¿Me hace el favor?
meh ah-theh ell fa-vor

Sorry
¡Perdón!
pair-don

I'm really sorry
Lo siento muchísimo
loh see-entoh mootchee-seemoh

Can you help me?
¿Puede ayudarme?
pweh-deh ayoodarmeh

Can you tell me...?
¿Puede decirme...?
pweh-deh detheer-meh

Can I have...?
¿Me da...?
meh da

I would like...
Quería...
keh-ree-a

Is there ... here?
¿Hay ... aquí?
I ... akee

Where are the toilets?
¿Dónde están los servicios?
dondeh esstan loss sair-veeth-yoss

Where can I get...?
¿Dónde puedo conseguir...?
dondeh pweh-doh konsegeer

How much is it?
¿Cuánto es?
kwantoh ess

Do you take credit cards?
¿Aceptan tarjeta de crédito?
atheptan tar-Heh-ta deh creditoh

Can I pay by cheque?
¿Puedo pagar con cheque?
pweh-doh pagar kon cheh-keh

What time is it?
¿Qué hora es?
keh ora ess

USEFUL EVERYDAY PHRASES

I must go now
Tengo que irme ya
teng-goh keh eermeh ya

Cheers!
¡Salud!
saloo

Go away!
¡Lárguese!
largheh-seh

THINGS YOU'LL SEE OR HEAR

abierto	open
agua potable	drinking water
ascensor	lift
aseos	toilets
caballeros	Gentlemen
caja	till
cerrado	closed
cerrado por vacaciones	closed for holiday period
empujar	Push
entrada	way in/entrance
entrada libre	admission free
entre sin llamar	enter without knocking
horas de visita	visiting hours
horas de oficina	opening times
lavabos	toilets
liquidación	sale
ocupado	engaged
privado	private
rebajas	sales

recién pintado	wet paint
reservado	reserved
saldos	sales
salida	way out
salida de emergencia	emergency exit
se alquila piso	flat for rent
se prohíbe la entrada	no admittance
se vende	for sale
Señoras	ladies
servicios	toilets
silencio	silence/quiet
tirar	Pull
ventanilla	window
¡Adelante!	Come in!
¿Cómo está usted?	How do you do?
De nada	Don't mention it
¡Encantado!	Pleased to meet you!
Gracias	Thank you
No	No
No hablo inglés	I don't speak English
No importa	Never mind/It doesn't matter
¡Perdón!	Sorry!
Por favor	Please
Sí	Yes
Vale	O.K.

DAYS, MONTHS, SEASONS

Sunday	domingo	*domeengoh*
Monday	lunes	*looness*
Tuesday	martes	*martess*
Wednesday	miércoles	*mee-airkoh-less*
Thursday	jueves	*Hweh-vess*
Friday	viernes	*vee-airness*
Saturday	sábado	*sabbadoh*
January	enero	*enneh-roh*
February	febrero	*febreh-roh*
March	marzo	*marthoh*
April	abril	*abreel*
May	mayo	*mayyoh*
June	junio	*Hoon-yoh*
July	julio	*Hool-yoh*
August	agosto	*agosstoh*
September	septiembre	*set-yembreh*
October	octubre	*oktoobreh*
November	noviembre	*nov-yembreh*
December	diciembre	*deeth-yembreh*
Spring	primavera	*preema-veh-ra*
Summer	verano	*verah-noh*
Autumn	otoño	*otone-yoh*
Winter	invierno	*eemb-yairnoh*
Christmas	Navidad	*navee-da*
Christmas Eve	Nochebuena	*notcheh-bweh-na*
Easter	Pascua, Semana Santa	*paskwa, semah-na santa*
Good Friday	Viernes Santo	*vee-airness santoh*
New Year	Año Nuevo	*ahn-yoh nweh-voh*
New Year's Eve	Nochevieja	*notcheh-vee-eh-Ha*

NUMBERS

0 cero *theh-roh*
1 uno, una *oonoh, oona*
2 dos *doss*
3 tres *tress*
4 cuatro *kwatroh*

5 cinco *theenkoh*
6 seis *sayss*
7 siete *see-eh-teh*
8 ocho *otchoh*
9 nueve *nweh-veh*

10 diez *dee-eth*
11 once *ontheh*
12 doce *doh-theh*
13 trece *treh-theh*
14 catorce *katortheh*
15 quince *keentheh*
16 dieciséis *dee-ethee-sayss*
17 diecisiete *dee-ethee-see-eh-teh*
18 dieciocho *dee-ethee-otchoh*
19 diecinueve *dee-ethee-nweh-veh*
20 veinte *vainteh*
21 veintiuno *vaintee-oonoh*
22 veintidós *vaintee-doss*
30 treinta *trainta*
31 treinta y uno *traintI oonoh*
32 treinta y dos *traintI doss*
40 cuarenta *kwarenta*
50 cincuenta *theen-kwenta*
60 sesenta *sessenta*
70 setenta *setenta*
80 ochenta *otchenta*
90 noventa *noh-venta*
100 cien *thee-enn*
110 ciento diez *thee-entoh dee-eth*
200 doscientos/doscientas *dosthee-entoss/dossthee-entass*
1000 mil *meel*
1,000,000 un millón *meel-yon*

13

TIME

today	hoy	*oy*
yesterday	ayer	*ayyair*
tomorrow	mañana	*man-yah-na*
the day before yesterday	anteayer	*anteh-ayyair*
the day after tomorrow	pasado mañana	*passah-doh man-yah-na*
this week	esta semana	*essta semah-na*
last week	la semana pasada	*la semah-na passah-da*
next week	la semana que viene	*la semah-na keh vee-eh-neh*
this morning	esta mañana	*essta man-yah-na*
this afternoon	esta tarde	*essta tardeh*
this evening	esta tarde/noche	*essta tardeh/notcheh*
tonight	esta noche	*essta notcheh*
yesterday afternoon	ayer por la tarde	*ayyair por la tardeh*
last night	anoche	*annotcheh*
tomorrow morning	mañana por la mañana	*man-yah-na por la man-yah-na*
tomorrow night	mañana por la noche	*man-yah-na por la notcheh*
in three days	dentro de tres días	*dentroh deh tress dee-ass*
three days ago	hace tres días	*ah-theh tress dee-ass*
late	tarde	*tardeh*
early	temprano	*temprah-noh*
soon	pronto	*prontoh*
later on	más tarde	*mass tardeh*
at the moment	en este momento	*en essteh momentoh*
second	un segundo	*segoondoh*
minute	un minuto	*meenootoh*
ten minutes	diez minutos	*dee-eth meenootoss*
quarter of an hour	un cuarto de hora	*kwartoh deh ora*

half an hour	media hora	*maid-ya ora*
three quarters of an hour	tres cuartos de hora	*tress kwartoss deh ora*
hour	la hora	*ora*
day	el día	*dee-a*
week	la semana	*semah-na*
fortnight, 2 weeks	la quincena	*keentheh-na*
month	el mes	*mess*
year	el año	*ahn-yoh*

TELLING THE TIME

In Spanish you always put the hour first, then the word *y* (denoting 'and', for 'past' the hour) or *menos* ('less', for 'to' the hour) followed by the minutes — i.e. 5.20 = 5 and 20 = *las 5 y 20*; 5.40 = 20 to 6 = *las 6 menos 20*. The 24 hour clock is used officially in timetables and enquiry offices.

one o'clock	la una	*la oona*
ten past one	la una y diez	*la oona ee dee-eth*
quarter past one	la una y cuarto	*la oona ee kwartoh*
twenty past one	la una y veinte	*la oona ee vainteh*
half past one	la una y media	*la oona ee maid-ya*
twenty to two	las dos menos veinte	*lass doss meh-noss vainteh*
quarter to two	las dos menos cuarto	*lass doss meh-noss kwartoh*
ten to two	las dos menos diez	*lass doss meh-noss dee-eth*
two o'clock	las dos	*lass doss*
13.00 (1 pm)	las trece horas	*lass treh-theh orass*
16.30 (4.30 pm)	las dieciséis treinta	*lass dee-ethee-sayss trainta*

20.10 (8.10 pm)	las veinte diez	*lass vainteh dee-eth*
at half past five	a las cinco y media	*ah lass theenkoh ee maid-ya*
at seven o'clock	a las siete	*ah lass see-eh-teh*
noon	mediodía	*maid-yoh-dee-a*
midnight	medianoche	*maid-ya-notcheh*

HOTELS

Hotels are divided into 5 classes (star rating), followed by the *pensiones* which have three. Further down the scale comes the *hotel-residencia* for longer stays and the *hostal* which is similar to a *pensión*. An *albergue* is usually a country hotel situated in a picturesque area and is meant for short stays. The state-run *paradores* are superior (often converted castles, palaces etc.) and allow unlimited stays, though you will have to pay for the extra comfort and scenery. If travelling in the high season it is always advisable to book accommodation in advance in the more popular areas.

USEFUL WORDS AND PHRASES

balcony	el balcón	*bal-kon*
bathroom	el cuarto de baño	*kwartoh deh bahn-yoh*
bed	la cama	*kah-ma*
bedroom	la habitación	*abbee-tath-yon*
bill	la cuenta	*kwenta*
breakfast	el desayuno	*dessa-yoonoh*
dining room	el comedor	*kommeh-dor*
dinner	la cena	*theh-na*
double room	una habitación doble	*abbee-tath-yon doh-bleh*
foyer	el hall	*Hol*
full board	pensión completa	*penss-yon kompleh-ta*
half board	media pensión	*maid-ya penss-yon*
hotel	el hotel	*oh-tell*
key	la llave	*yah-veh*
lift, elevator	el ascensor	*ass-then-sor*
lounge	el salón	*sa-lonn*
lunch	la comida	*komee-da*
manager	el director	*deerek-tor*
receipt	la factura	*fak-toora*
reception	la recepción	*reh-thepth-yon*
receptionist	el recepcionista	*reh-thepth-yoneessta*

restaurant	el restaurante	*resstow-ranteh*
room	la habitación	*abbee-tath-yon*
room service	el servicio de	*sairveeth-yoh deh*
	habitaciones	*abbeetath-yoh-ness*
shower	la ducha	*dootcha*
single room	una habitación	*abbee-tath-yon*
	individual	*eendeeveed-wal*
toilet	el wáter	*vattair*
twin room	una habitación con	*abbee-tath-yon kon doss*
	dos camas	*kah-mass*

Have you any vacancies?
¿Tienen alguna habitación libre?
tee-eh-nen algoona abbee-tath-yon lee-breh

I have a reservation
He hecho una reserva
eh etcho oona reh-sairva

I'd like a single/double room
Quería una habitación individual/doble
keh-ree-a oona abbee-tath-yon eendeeveed-wal/dobleh

I'd like a twin room
Quería una habitación con dos camas
ker-ree-a oona abbee-tath-yon kon doss kah-mass

I'd like a room with a bathroom/balcony
Quería una habitación con cuarto de baño/con balcón
keh-ree-a oona abbee-tath-yon kon kwartoh deh bahn-yoh/kon bal-konn

I'd like a room for one night/three nights
Quería una habitación para una noche/para tres noches
keh-ree-a oona abbee-tath-yon parra oona notcheh/parra tress notchess

What is the charge per night?
¿Cuál es la tarifa por noche?
kwal ess la tarreefa por notcheh

REPLIES YOU MAY BE GIVEN

Lo siento, está lleno
I'm sorry, we're full

No nos quedan habitaciones individuales/dobles
There are no single/double rooms left

Completo
No vacancies

Haga el favor de pagar por adelantado
Please pay in advance

I don't know yet how long I'll stay
Todavía no sé cuánto tiempo me voy a quedar
todavee-a noh seh kwantoh tee-empoh meh voy ah keh-dar

When is breakfast/dinner?
¿A qué hora es el desayuno/la cena?
ah keh ora ess el dessa-yoonoh/la theh-na

Would you have my luggage brought up, please?
¿Puede hacer que me suban el equipaje, por favor?
pweh-deh athair keh meh sooban el ekee-pah-Heh, por fa-vor

Please call me at ... o'clock
Haga el favor de llamarme a las...
ah-ga el fa-vor deh yamar-meh ah lass

Can I have breakfast in my room?
¿Pueden servirme el desayuno en mi habitación?
pweh-den sair-veermeh el dessa-yoonoh en mee abbee-tath-yon

I'll be back at ... o'clock
Volveré a las...
volveh-reh ah lass

My room number is...
El número de mi habitación es el...
el noomeh-roh deh mee abbee-tath-yon ess

I'm leaving tomorrow
Me marcho mañana
meh marcho man-yah-na

Can I have the bill please?
¿Me da la cuenta, por favor?
meh da la kwenta, por fa-vor

Can you get me a taxi?
¿Puede llamar a un taxi?
pweh-deh yamar ah oon taksee

Can you recommend another hotel?
¿Puede recomendar otro hotel?
pweh-deh rekomendar otroh oh-tell

THINGS YOU'LL SEE OR HEAR

almuerzo	lunch
ascensor	lift, elevator
baño	bath
botones	bell boy
cena	dinner
comida	lunch, meal
cuenta	bill
desayuno	breakfast
dormir y desayunar	bed and breakfast
ducha	shower
empujar	push
habitación doble	double room
habitación individual	single room
media pensión	half board
pensión completa	full board
planta baja	ground floor
recepción	reception
reserva	reservation
restaurante	restaurant
salida de emergencia	emergency exit
servicio	toilet
telefonista	switchboard operator
tirar	pull
wáter	toilet

CAMPING AND CARAVANNING

There are plenty of recognized sites all over Spain, especially along the Mediterranean coast, and most are open all year round. Outside these sites you will need a permit from landowners or authorities such as the Forestry Authority – ask the Spanish Tourist Office for details.

Youth hostels are open to members of the YHA, but in the high season it is best to book in advance and stays are limited to 3 nights – details from the Spanish Tourist Office in London or local offices in Spain.

USEFUL WORDS AND PHRASES

bucket	el cubo	koo-boh
campsite	un camping	kampeen
campfire	una hoguera	oh-gheh-ra
to go camping	ir de camping	eer deh kampeen
caravan	la caravana	karavah-na
caravan site	un camping	kampeen
cooking utensils	los utensilios de cocina	ootenseel-yoss deh kotheena
drinking water	agua potable	ahg-wa pottah-bleh
ground sheet	la lona impermeable	loh-na eempair-meh-ah-bleh
to hitch-hike	hacer auto-stop	athair owtoh-stop
rope	una cuerda	kwairda
rubbish	la basura	bassoora
rucksack	la mochila	motcheela
saucepans	las cazuelas	kath-weh-lass
sleeping bag	el saco de dormir	sah-koh deh dormeer
tent	la tienda	tee-enda
trailer (R.V.)	la caravana	karavah-na
youth hostel	un albergue juvenil	albair-gheh Hooveneel

Can I camp here?
¿Puedo acampar aquí?
pweh-doh akampar akee

Can we park the caravan here?
¿Podemos aparcar aquí la caravana?
podeh-moss aparkar akee la karavah-na

Where is the nearest campsite/caravan site?
¿Dónde está el camping más cercano?
dondeh essta el kampeen mass thair-kah-noh

What is the charge per night?
¿Cuál es la tarifa por noche?
kwal ess la tareefa por notcheh

What facilities are there?
¿Qué instalaciones hay?
keh eensta-lath-yoness I

Can I light a fire here?
¿Puedo encender fuego aquí?
pweh-doh enthen-dair fweh-go akee

Where can I get...?
¿Dónde puedo conseguir...?
dondeh pweh-doh konseh-gheer

Is there drinking water here?
¿Hay agua potable aquí?
I ahg-wa pottah-bleh akee

CAMPING AND CARAVANNING

THINGS YOU'LL SEE OR HEAR

agua potable	drinking water
albergue juvenil	youth hostel
aseos	toilet
camping	campsite
caravana	caravan, trailer (R.V.)
carnet	pass, identity card
cocina	kitchen
ducha	shower
fuego	fire
luz	light
manta	blanket
prestar	to lend
prohibido acampar	no camping
remolque	trailer (camping etc.)
saco de dormir	sleeping bag
tarifa	charges
tienda	tent
uso	use
wáter	toilet

MOTORING

More motorways are being built in Spain, but they can be expensive to use because of the tolls. The best roads to use are the national highways *(nacionales)* as they often have crawler lanes for heavy vehicles, especially on gradients, which makes overtaking much easier. There are few dual-lane highways. Secondary roads *(comarcales)* are not so good and can often be in quite poor condition. When using a map, the routes coloured green or red are the major ones, the yellow are secondary and the white routes are best left to the adventurous.

The rule of the road is: Drive on the right, overtake on the left. There are no priority rules such as in France, since all secondary roads give way to major routes at junctions and crossroads. In the case of roads having equal status, or at unmarked junctions, traffic coming from the RIGHT has priority. A system worth noting for changing direction or for crossing over dual-lane highways is a semi-circular slip road (which is not always sign-posted).

The speed limit on national highways is 100 km/h (62 mph), otherwise keep to the speed shown. In built up areas the limit will vary between 40 km/h and 60 km/h (25-35 mph). Equipment to be carried at all times includes a spare set of bulbs and a red triangle in case of breakdown or accidents. The Traffic Police patrols *(Guardia Civil de Tráfico)* will help you if in trouble, just as they will be ready to fine you on the spot should you infringe the law!

Petrol stations on the highways are usually open 24 hours a day, but elsewhere they close late at night. Fuel ratings are as follows:
** = normal
*** = super
**** = extra
diesel fuel = gas-oil

SOME COMMON ROAD SIGNS

aduana	customs
apagar luces de cruce	headlights off
aparcamiento	car park
atención al tren	beware of the trains
autopista (de peaje)	motorway (with toll)
calzada deteriorada	bad surface
calzada irregular	uneven surface
calle peatonal	pedestrian precinct
ceda el paso	give way
centro ciudad	town centre
cruce	crossroads
cruce peligroso	dangerous junction
cuidado	watch out
curva peligrosa	dangerous bend
despacio	slow
desvío	diversion
dirección prohibida	no entry
dirección única	one-way street
encender luces de cruce	headlights on
escuela	school
estacionamento limitado	restricted parking
estación de servicio	service station
final de autopista	end of motorway
firme en mal estado	bad surface
garaje	garage
gasolina	petrol, fuel
gasolinera	filling station
obras	roadworks
ojo al tren	beware of the trains
paso a nivel	level crossings
paso de ganado	cattle crossing
paso subterráneo	pedestrian underpass
peaje	toll

peatón, circula por tu izquierda	pedestrian, keep to the left
peatones	pedestrians
peligro	danger
precaución	caution
prohibido adelantar	no overtaking
prohibido el paso	no tresspassing
puesto de socorro	first aid
salida de camiones	lorries, trucks turning
taller (de reparaciones)	garage
vado permanente	in constant use (no parking)
vehículos pesados	for heavy vehicles
zona azul	restricted parking zone

USEFUL WORDS AND PHRASES

bonnet	el capó	*kapo*
boot	el maletero	*malleh-teh-roh*
breakdown	una avería	*avveh-ree-ah*
brake	el freno	*freh-noh*
car	el coche	*kotcheh*
caravan	la caravana	*karra-vah-na*
crossroads	el cruce	*kroo-theh*
to drive	conducir	*kondoo-theer*
engine	el motor	*moh-tor*
exhaust	el tubo de escape	*tooboh deh esskah-peh*
fanbelt	la correa del ventilador	*korreh-ah del venteela-dor*
garage		
(for repairs)	un taller/garaje	*tayyair/garah-Heh*
(for fuel)	una gasolinera	*gassoh-leeneh-ra*
gasoline	la gasolina	*gassoh-leena*
gear	la marcha	*marcha*
gears	las marchas	*mar-chass*

hood	el capó	*kapo*
junction (on motorway)	un enlace	*enlah-theh*
licence	el carnet	*kar-neh*
lights *(head)*	las luces de cruce	*loothess deh krootheh*
(rear)	las luces traseras	*loothess trasseh-rass*
lorry	el camión	*kam-yon*
mirror	el (espejo) retrovisor	*esspeh-Hoh retroh-veessor*
motorbike	la motocicleta	*motoh-thee-kleh-ta*
motorway	la autopista	*owtoh-peessta*
number plate	la matrícula	*matree-koola*
petrol	la gasolina	*gassoh-leena*
road	la carretera	*karreh-teh-ra*
to skid	patinar	*patee-nar*
spares	los repuestos	*reh-pwesstoss*
speed	la velocidad	*velothee-da*
speed limit	el límite de velocidad	*leemeeteh deh velothee-da*
speedometer	el cuentakilómetros	*kwenta-keelommeh-tross*
steering wheel	el volante	*voh-lanteh*
tire, tyre	el neumático	*neh-oo-matikoh*
to tow	remolcar	*reh-molkar*
traffic lights	el semáforo	*seh-mafforoh*
trailer	el remolque	*reh-molkeh*
trailer (R.V.)	la caravana	*karra-vah-nah*
truck	el camión	*kam-yon*
trunk	el maletero	*malleh-teh-roh*
van	la furgoneta	*foorgoneh-ta*
wheel	la rueda	*roo-weh-da*
windscreen/shield	el parabrisas	*parra-bree-sass*

I'd like some fuel/oil/water
Quería gasolina/aceite/agua
keh-ree-a gassoh-leena/athay-teh/ahg-wa

Fill her up please!
¡Lleno, por favor!
yeh-noh, por fa-vor

I'd like 10 litres of fuel, please
Póngame diez litros, por favor
ponga-meh dee-eth leetross, por fa-vor

Would you check the tires please?
¿Podría revisar los neumáticos, por favor?
podree-a revee-sarmeh loss neh-oo-matikoss, por fa-vor

Where is the nearest garage?
¿Dónde está el taller más cercano?
dondeh essta el tayair mass thair-kah-noh

How do I get to...?
¿Cómo se va a...?
koh-moh seh va ah

Is this the road to...?
¿Es ésta la carretera de...?
ess essta la karreh-teh-ra deh

DIRECTIONS YOU MAY BE GIVEN

todo derecho	straight on
a la izquierda	on the left
tuerza a la izquierda	turn left
a la derecha	on the right
tuerza a la derecha	turn right
la primera a la derecha	first on the right
la segunda a la izquierda	second on the left
después de pasar el/la...	go past the...

Do you do repairs?
¿Hacen reparaciones?
ah-then reparrath-yoness

Can you repair the clutch?
¿Pueden arreglarme el embrague?
pweh-den arreh-glarmeh el embrah-gheh

How long will it take?
¿Cuánto tiempo les llevará?
kwantoh tee-empoh less yeh-vara

There is something wrong with the engine
Hay algo que no va bien en el motor
I algoh keh no va bee-en en el moh-tor

The engine is overheating
El motor se calienta demasiado
el moh-tor seh kal-yenta deh-massee-ah-doh

The brakes are slipping
Los frenos no agarran
loss freh-noss no agarran

I need a new tire
Necesito un neumático nuevo
neh-thessee-toh oon neh-oo-matikoh nweh-voh

I'd like to hire a car
Quería alquilar un coche
keh-ree-a alkee-lar oon kotcheh

Where can I park?
¿Dónde puedo aparcar?
dondeh pweh-doh appar-kar

Can I park here?
¿Puedo aparcar aquí?
pweh-doh appar-kar akee

THINGS YOU'LL SEE OR HEAR

aceite	oil
atasco	traffic jam
autopista	motorway
autopista de peaje	motorway with toll
calzada para camiones	crawler lane
cola	queue
desvío	diversion
enlace (de autopista)	motorway junction
extra	4 star
gas-oil	diesel
gasolina	petrol, fuel
gasolinera	filling station
limpiaparabrisas	windscreen/shield wiper
nivel del aceite	oil level
normal	2 star
presión	air pressure
presión de los neumáticos	tire pressure
reparación	repair
salida	exit
super	3 star

RAIL TRAVEL

Spanish trains are slow when compared to coaches, even between major cities, but they are reasonably comfortable. The main types of train are:

TALGO, TER	Fast diesel trains with air-conditioning; a supplement is required on top of the normal fare.
TAF	Slower diesel express used on secondary routes.
Exprés	A misleading name, as this is a slow night train stopping at all stations
Rápido	Also misleading as it is just a daytime version of the *exprés*.
Automotor Tranvía Omnibús Ferrobús	Local short-distance trains.

USEFUL WORDS AND PHRASES

booking office	el despacho de billetes	*dess-patchoh deh beeyeh-tess*
buffet	la cafetería	*kaffeh-teh-ree-a*
carriage, car	el vagón	*va-gon*
compartment	el compartimento	*kompartee-mentoh*
connection	una conexión	*konneks-yon*
currency exchange	el cambio de moneda	*kamb-yoh deh monneh-da*
dining car	el vagón-comedor	*va-gon kommeh-dor*
emergency cord	la alarma	*alar-ma*
engine	la máquina	*makee-na*
entrance	la entrada	*entrah-da*
exit	la salida	*salee-da*

first class	primera clase	*preemeh-ra klah-seh*
to get in	entrar	*entrar*
to get out	salir	*saleer*
guard	el guarda	*gwar-da*
indicator board	el tablero de información	*tableh-roh deh eemfor-math-yon*
left luggage	la consigna	*konseeg-na*
lost property	objetos perdidos	*ob-Heh-toss pairdee-doss*
luggage rack	la rejilla de equipajes	*reh-Hee-ya deh ekee-pah-Hess*
luggage trolley	un carrito para el equipaje	*karree-toh parra ell ekee-pah-Heh*
luggage van	el furgón de equipajes	*foor-gon deh ekee-pah-Hess*
platform	el andén	*an-den*
rail	un raíl	*rah-eel*
railway	el ferrocarril	*ferroh-karreel*
reserved seat	un asiento reservado	*ass-yentoh reh-sair-vah-doh*
restaurant car	el vagón-restaurante	*va-gon resstow-ranteh*
return ticket	un billete de ida y vuelta	*bee-yeh-teh deh eeda ee vwel-ta*
seat	un asiento	*ass-yentoh*
second class	segunda clase	*segoonda klah-seh*
single ticket	un billete de ida	*beeyeh-teh deh eeda*
sleeping car	el coche-cama	*kotcheh kah-ma*
station	la estación	*esstath-yon*
station master	el jefe de estación	*Heh-feh deh esstath-yon*
ticket	un billete	*beeyeh-teh*
ticket collector	el revisor	*reh-vee-sor*
timetable	el horario	*oh-rar-yoh*
tracks	las vías	*vee-ass*
train	el tren	*tren*
waiting room	la sala de espera	*sah-la deh espeh-ra*
window	la ventana	*ventah-na*

33

When does the train for ... leave?
¿A qué hora sale el tren para...?
ah keh ora sah-leh el tren parra

When does the train from ... arrive?
¿A qué hora llega el tren de...?
ah keh ora yeh-ga el tren deh

When is the next/first/last train to...?
¿A qué hora sale el próximo/primer/último tren para...?
ah keh ora sah-leh el prok-seemoh/preemair/ool-teemoh tren parra

What is the fare to...?
¿Cuál es la tarifa para...?
kwal ess la tarree-fa parra

Do I have to change?
¿Tengo que hacer transbordo?
teng-goh keh athair tranz-bordoh

Does the train stop at...?
¿Para el tren en...?
pah-ra el tren en

How long does it take to get to...?
¿Cuánto tiempo se tarda en llegar a...?
kwantoh tee-em-poh seh tar-da en yeh-gar ah

A single/return ticket to ... please
Un billete/un billete de ida y vuelta a ... por favor
oon beeyeh-teh/oon beeyeh-teh deh eeda ee vwel-ta ah ... por fa-vor

Do I have to pay a supplement?
¿Tengo que pagar suplemento?
teng-goh keh pagar soopleh-mentoh

I'd like to reserve a seat
Quería reservar un asiento
keh-ree-ah reh-sair-var oon ass-yentoh

Is this the right train for...?
¿Es éste el tren para...?
ess essteh el tren parra

Is this the right platform for the ... train?
¿Es éste el andén para el tren de...?
ess essteh el anden parra el tren deh

Which platform for the ... train?
¿Qué andén para el tren de...?
keh anden parra el tren deh

Is the train late?
¿Lleva retraso el tren?
yeh-va reh-trah-soh el tren

Could you help me with my luggage please?
¿Puede ayudarme con estas maletas, por favor?
pweh-deh ayoodar-meh kon esstass maleh-tass por fa-vor

Is this a non-smoking compartment?
¿Está prohibido fumar aquí?
essta pro-ee-beedoh foomar akee

Is this seat free?
¿Está libre este asiento?
essta leebreh essteh ass-yentoh

This seat is taken
Este asiento está ocupado
essteh ass-yentoh essta okoopah-doh

I have reserved this seat
Tengo reservado este asiento
teng-goh reh-sairvah-doh essteh ass-yentoh

May I open/close the window?
¿Puedo abrir/cerrar la ventana?
pweh-doh abreer/therrar la ventah-na

When do we arrive in...?
¿A qué hora llegamos a...?
ah keh ora yeh-gah-moss ah

What station is this?
¿Qué estación es ésta?
keh esstath-yon ess essta

Do we stop at...?
¿Paramos en...?
parah-moss en

Would you keep an eye on my things for a moment?
¿Podría usted guardarme las cosas un momento?
podree-ah ooss-teh gwar-darmeh lass koh-sass oon momentoh

Is there a restaurant car on this train?
¿Lleva vagón-restaurante este tren?
yeh-va va-gon resstow-ranteh essteh tren

THINGS YOU'LL SEE OR HEAR

alarma	emergency alarm
a los andenes	to the trains
andén	platform
atención	attention
bajar	to get off
billete de andén	platform ticket
billetes	tickets, ticket office
bocadillos	snacks
cambio de moneda	currency exchange
coche-cama	sleeping car
consigna	left luggage
demora	delay
Días Azules	cheap travel days
domingos y festivos	Sundays and public holidays
entrada	entrance
equipajes	left luggage
estación principal	central station
excepto domingos	Sundays excepted
fumadores	smokers
horario	timetable
información	information
libre	vacant
llegadas	arrivals
multa por uso indebido	penalty for misuse
no para en...	does not stop in...
ocupado	engaged
prensa	newspaper kiosk
prohibido asomarse a la ventana	do not lean out of the window
prohibido el paso	no entry
prohibido fumar	no smoking
prohibida la entrada	no entry
puesto de periódicos	newspaper kiosk

→

RENFE	Spanish national railways
reserva de asientos	seat reservation
retirarse	to stand back
retraso	delay
sala de espera	waiting room
salida	exit
salidas	departures
sólo laborables	weekdays only
subir	to get in
suplemento	supplement
taquilla	ticket office
tren de cercanías	local train
vagón	carriage, car
viaje	journey

AIR TRAVEL

Numerous international airlines provide services to the following
Spanish destinations: Madrid, Barcelona, Bilbao, Valencia, Alicante,
Malaga, Seville, Santiago, Tenerife in the Canaries, and Palma,
Menorca and Ibiza in the Balearic Islands. There is also a domestic
network connecting the main cities in Spain.

USEFUL WORDS AND PHRASES

aircraft	el avión	av-yon
air hostess	la azafata	atha-fah-ta
airline	la compañía aérea	kompan-yee-a ah-aireh-a
airport	el aeropuerto	ah-airoh-pwair-toh
airport bus	el autobús del aeropuerto	owtoh-booss del ah-airoh-pwair-toh
aisle	el pasillo	pasee-yo
arrivals	llegadas	yeh-gah-dass
baggage claim	reclamación	reh-klamath-yon
boarding card	la tarjeta de embarque	tar-Heh-ta deh embarkeh
check-in	la facturación	faktoorath-yon
check-in desk	el mostrador de facturación	mosstra-dor deh faktoorath-yon
delay	retraso	reh-trah-soh
departure	la salida	saleeda
departure lounge	salidas	saleedass
emergency exit	la salida de emergencia	saleeda deh eh-mair-Henth-ya
flight	el vuelo	vveh-loh
flight number	el número de vuelo	noomeh-roh deh vveh-loh
gate	la puerta (de embarque)	pwair-ta deh embar-keh

39

jet	el reactor	*reh-aktor*
land	aterrizar	*aterree-thar*
passport	el pasaporte	*passa-porteh*
passport control	el control de pasaportes	*kontrol deh passa-portess*
pilot	el piloto	*peeloh-toh*
runway	la pista	*peess-ta*
seat	un asiento	*ass-yentoh*
seat belt	el cinturón de seguridad	*theentoo-ron deh segooree-da*
steward	el aeromozo	*ah-airoh-moh-thoh*
stewardess	la azafata	*atha-fah-ta*
take off	despegar	*desspeh-gar*
window	la ventanilla	*ventanee-ya*
wing	el ala	*ah-la*

When is there a flight to...?
¿A qué hora hay vuelo para...?
ah keh ora I vweh-loh parra

What time does the flight to ... leave?
¿A qué hora sale el vuelo para...?
ah keh ora sah-leh el vweh-loh parra

Is it a direct flight?
¿Es un vuelo directo?
ess oon vweh-loh deerek-toh

Do I have to change planes?
¿Tengo que hacer transbordo?
teng-goh keh athair tranz-bordoh

When do I have to check in?
¿A qué hora tengo que hacer la facturación?
ah keh ora teng-goh keh athair la faktoorath-yon

I'd like a single/return ticket to...
Quería un billete (de ida)/un billete de ida y vuelta para...
keh-ree-a oon beeyeh-teh (deh eeda)/oon beeyeh-teh deh eeda ee vwelta parra

I'd like a non-smoking seat please
Quería un asiento en la sección de no fumadores, por favor
keh-ree-a oon ass-yentoh en la sekth-yon deh no fooma-doress, por fa-vor

I'd like a window seat please
Quería un asiento junto a la ventanilla, por favor
keh-ree-a oon ass-yentoh ah la ventanee-ya, por fa-vor

How long will the flight be delayed?
¿Cuánto retraso lleva el vuelo?
kwantoh reh-trah-soh yeh-va el vweh-loh

Is this the right gate for the ... flight?
¿Es ésta la puerta de embarque del vuelo de...?
ess essta la pwair-ta deh embarkeh del vweh-loh deh

When do we arrive in...?
¿A qué hora llegamos a...?
ah keh ora yeh-gah-moss ah

May I smoke now?
¿Puedo fumar ya?
pweh-doh foomar yah

I do not feel very well
No me encuentro muy bien
no meh enkwen-troh mwee bee-en

THINGS YOU'LL SEE OR HEAR

abróchense el cinturón	fasten seat belt
abstenerse de fumar	no smoking please
aduana	customs control
aeromozo	steward
altitud	altitude
aterrizaje	landing
aterrizaje de emergencia	emergency landing
avión	aircraft
azafata	stewardess
comandante	captain
control de pasaportes	passport control
despegue	take-off
escala	intermediate stop
escalerilla	steps
facturación	check-in
facturar	to check in
hora local	local time
información	information
llegadas	arrivals
no fumadores	non-smokers
pasajeros	passengers
pista	runway
puerta de embarque	gate
reclamación	baggage claim
retraso	delay
salida de emergencia	emergency exit
salidas	departures
velocidad	speed
vuelo	flight
vuelo directo	direct flight
vuelo regular	scheduled flight

BUS, METRO & BOAT TRAVEL

All Spanish cities have a good bus network. Most buses are one-man operated and you pay the driver as you enter. Since there is generally a flat fare, it is cheaper to buy a book of tickets called a *bonobús* and there are also other types of runabout ticket.

Both Madrid and Barcelona have an underground (subway) system, the *metro*. Again, a flat fare is in operation and you can buy a *taco* (book of tickets) or a 7-day ticket giving unlimited travel.

There is an excellent coach network covering the whole of Spain, giving better connecting service between cities and covering the gaps in the railway system. The coaches are comfortable and fast, and have facilities such as video and air-conditioning (essential in a hot climate).

There is a daily boat service to the Balearics (usually overnight) and a less frequent service to the Canaries, taking about 2 days. There is also a daily ferry linking Algeciras to North African ports such as Tangiers, Ceuta and Melilla.

Taxis display a green light at night, and a sign in the windscreen says if they are for hire *(libre)*.

USEFUL WORDS AND PHRASES

adult	un adulto	*adool-toh*
boat	el barco	*barkoh*
bus	el autobús	*owtoh-booss*
bus stop	la parada del autobús	*parrah-da del owtoh-booss*
child	un niño	*neen-yoh*
coach	el autocar	*owtoh-kar*
conductor	el cobrador	*kobra-dor*
connection	la conexión	*konneks-yon*
cruise	un crucero	*krootheh-roh*
driver	el conductor	*kondook-tor*
fare	el billete	*beeyeh-teh*
ferry	el ferry	*ferree*

43

lake	un lago	*lah-goh*
network map	un plano	*plah-noh*
number 5 bus	el (autobús número) cinco	*owtoh-booss noomeh-roh theeng-koh*
passenger	un pasajero	*passa-Heh-roh*
port	el puerto	*pwair-toh*
quay	el muelle	*mwell-yeh*
river	el río	*ree-oh*
sea	el mar	*mar*
seat	un asiento	*ass-yentoh*
ship	el barco	*barkoh*
station	la estación	*esstath-yon*
terminus	la terminal	*tairmee-nal*
ticket	un billete	*beeyeh-teh*
underground, subway	el metro	*meh-troh*

Where is the nearest underground (subway) station?
¿Dónde está la estación de metro más cercana?
dondeh essta la esstath-yon deh meh-troh mass thair-kah-na

Where is the bus station?
¿Dónde está la estación de autobuses?
dondeh essta la esstath-yon deh owtoh-boo-sess

Where is there a bus stop?
¿Dónde hay una parada de autobús?
dondeh I oona parrah-da deh owtoh-booss

Which buses go to...?
¿Qué autobuses van a...?
keh owtoh-boo-sess van ah

How often do the buses to ... run?
¿Cada cuánto tiempo pasan los autobuses para...?
kah-da kwantoh tee-em-poh pah-san loss owtoh-boo-sess parra

Would you tell me when we get to...?
¿Podría usted avisarme cuando lleguemos a...?
podree-a oosteh aveesar-meh kwando yeh-gheh-moss ah

Do I have to get off yet?
¿Tengo que bajarme ya?
teng-goh keh ba-Harmeh yah

How do you get to...?
¿Cómo se va a...?
koh-moh seh va ah

Is it very far?
¿Está muy lejos?
essta mwee leh-Hoss

Where can I get a taxi?
¿Dónde puedo tomar un taxi?
dondeh pweh-doh tomar oon taksee

I want to go to...
Quiero ir a...
kee-eh-roh eer ah

Do you go near...?
¿Pasa usted cerca de...?
pah-sa oosteh thair-ka deh

Where can I buy a ticket?
¿Dónde puedo sacar un billete?
dondeh pweh-doh sakar oon beeyeh-teh

Please close/open the window
¿Puede cerrar/abrir la ventana, por favor?
pweh-deh therrar/abreer la ventah-na, por fa-vor

Could you help me get a ticket?
¿Podría usted ayudarme a sacar un billete?
podree-a oosteh ayoo-darmeh ah sakar oon beeyeh-teh

When does the last bus leave?
¿A qué hora sale el último autobús?
ah keh ora sah-leh el ool-teemoh owtoh-booss

THINGS YOU'LL SEE OR HEAR

adultos	adults
asientos	seats
billete	ticket
bonobús	book of 10 bus tickets
completo	full
conductor	driver
enseñar	to show
entrada	entrance
entrada por delante/por detrás	entry at the front/rear
hacer transbordo	to change
niños	children
pagar	to pay
parada	stop
prohibido fumar	no smoking
prohibido hablar con el conductor	do not speak to the driver
prohibida la entrada	no entry
puerto	harbour
revisor	ticket inspector
ruta	route
salida	departure, exit
salida de emergencia	emergency exit
taco	book of metro tickets
terminal	terminus

RESTAURANT

You can eat in a variety of places:

Restaurante: These have an official rating (1-5 forks), but this depends more on the variety of dishes served than on the quality!

Cafetería: Not to be confused with the English term! It is a combined bar, cafe and restaurant. Service is provided at the counter or, for a little extra, at a table. There is usually a good variety of set menus at reasonable prices (look for *platos combinados*).

Fonda: Offers cheap, simple food which is usually good and representative of regional dishes.

Hostería or *Hostál:* A restaurant that usually specializes in regional dishes.

Parador: Belonging to the state-run hotels, they offer a first rate service in select surroundings.

Bar/Café: Both are general cafes selling all kinds of food and drink (again, they are not to be confused with English establishments of the same name). Well worth trying if you just want a quick snack. In some places they serve free 'tasters' *(tapas)* with alcoholic drinks. Full meals often available.

Merendero: Open-air cafe on the coast or in the country. Usually cheap and good value.

USEFUL WORDS AND PHRASES

beer	una cerveza	*thairveh-tha*
bill	la cuenta	*kwenta*
bottle	la botella	*boteyya*
bowl	un cuenco	*kweng-koh*
cake	un pastel	*passtell*
chef	el cocinero	*kothee-neh-roh*
coffee	el café	*kaffeh*
cup	la taza	*tah-tha*
fork	el tenedor	*tenneh-dor*
glass	el vaso	*vah-soh*
knife	el cuchillo	*kootchee-yoh*
menu	la carta	*karta*
milk	la leche	*letcheh*
plate	el plato	*plah-toh*
receipt	una factura	*faktoora*
sandwich	un sandwich	*sand-weetch*
serviette	la servilleta	*sairvee-yeh-ta*
snack	un bocadillo	*boh-kadee-yoh*
soup	la sopa	*soh-pa*
spoon	la cuchara	*kootchah-ra*
sugar	el azúcar	*athookar*
table	una mesa	*meh-sa*
tea	el té	*teh*
teaspoon	la cucharilla	*kootcha-reeya*
tip	una propina	*propeena*
waiter	el camarero	*kamma-reh-roh*
waitress	la camarera	*kamma-reh-ra*
water	el agua	*ahg-wa*
wine	el vino	*veenoh*
wine list	la carta de vinos	*karta deh veenoss*

A table for 1/2/3 please
Una mesa para una/dos/tres personas, por favor
oona meh-sa parra oona/doss/tress pairsoh-nass, por fa-vor

Can we see the menu/wine list?
¿Nos trae la carta/la carta de vinos?
noss trah-eh la karta/la karta deh veenoss

What would you recommend?
¿Qué recomendaría usted?
keh rekomenda-ree-a oosteh

I'd like...
Querría...
keh-ree-a

Just a cup of coffee, please
Un café nada más, por favor
oon kaffeh nah-da mass, por fa-vor

Waiter!/Waitress!
¡Camarero!/¡Señorita!
kamma-reh-roh/sen-yor-reeta

Can we have the bill please?
¿Nos trae la cuenta, por favor?
noss trah-eh la kwenta, por fa-vor

I only want a snack
Sólo quiero una comida ligera
soloh kee-eh-roh oona kommeeda lee-Heh-ra

Is there a set menu?
¿Hay plato del día?
I plah-toh dell dee-a

I didn't order this
No he pedido esto
noh eh pedeedoh esstoh

May we have some more...?
¿Nos trae más...?
noss trah-eh mass

The meal was very good, thank you
La comida ha sido muy buena, gracias
la kommeeda ah seedoh mwee bweh-na, grath-yass

My compliments to the chef!
¡Felicite al cocinero de mi parte!
felee-theeteh al kotheeneh-roh deh mee parteh

MENU GUIDE

aceitunas	olives
acelgas	saltwort
achicoria	chicory
aguacate	avocado
ahumados	smoked fish
ajo	garlic
albaricoques	apricots
albóndigas	meat balls
alcachofas	artichokes
alcachofas con jamón	artichokes with ham
alcachofas salteadas	sauté artichokes
alcachofas vinagreta	artichokes vinaigrette
alcaparras	capers
almejas	clams
almejas a la marinera	clams stewed in wine and parsley
almejas naturales	live clams
almendras	almonds
alubias con...	beans with...
ancas de rana	frogs' legs
anchoas	anchovies
anguila	eel
angulas	baby eels
anís	anis
arenque	herring
arroz a la cubana	rice with fried eggs and banana fritters
arroz a la valenciana	rice with sea food
arroz con leche	rice pudding
asados	roasts
atún	tuna
avellanas	hazelnuts
bacalao a la vizcaína	cod served with ham, peppers and chilis
bacalao al pil pil	cod served with chilis and garlic
batido de chocolate	chocolate milk shake
batido de fresas	strawberry milk shake
batido de frutas	fruit milk shake
batido de vainilla	vanilla milk shake

bebidas	drinks
berenjenas	aubergines
berza	cabbage
besugo al horno	baked sea bream
bistec de ternera	veal steak
bizcochos	sponge fingers
bonito al horno	baked tuna fish
bonito con tomate	tuna with tomato
boquerones fritos	fried anchovies
brandy	brandy
brazo de gitano	swiss roll
brevas	figs
broqueta de riñones	kidney kebabs
buñuelos	light fried pastries
butifarra	Catalan sausage
cabrito asado	roast kid
cachelada	pork stew with eggs, tomato and onion
café	coffee
café con leche	white coffee
calabacines	courgettes/marrow
calabaza	pumpkin
calamares a la romana	squid rings in batter
calamares en su tinta	squid cooked in their ink
calamares fritos	fried squid
caldeirada	fish soup
caldereta gallega	vegetable stew
caldo de...	... soup
caldo de gallina	chicken soup
caldo de pescado	clear soup made with fish
caldo gallego	vegetable soup
caldo guanche	soup made with potatoes, onions, tomatoes and courgettes
callos a la madrileña	tripe cooked with chilis
camarones	baby prawns
canelones	canneloni
cangrejos de río	river crabs
caracoles	snails
caramelos	sweets
carnes	meats
carro de queso	cheese board

castañas...	... chestnuts
cebolla	onion
cebolletas	spring onions
centollo	spider crab
cerezas	cherries
cerveza	beer
cesta de frutas	a selection of fresh fruit
champiñón a la crema	mushrooms with cream sauce
champiñón a la plancha	grilled mushrooms
champiñón al ajillo	mushrooms with garlic
champiñón salteado	sauté mushrooms
chanquetes	fish *(similar to whitebait)*
chateaubrian	chateaubriand steak
chipirones	squid
chipirones en su tinta	squid cooked in their ink
chipirones rellenos	stuffed squid
chirimoyas	custard apples
chocos	squid
chuleta de buey	beef chop
chuleta de cerdo	pork chop
chuleta de cerdo empanada	breaded pork chop
chuleta de cordero	lamb chop
chuleta de ternera	veal chop
chuleta de ternera empanada	breaded veal chop
chuletas de cordero empanadas	breaded lamb chops
chuletas de lomo ahumado	smoked pork chops
chuletitas de cordero	small lamb chops
chuletón	large chop
chuletón de buey	large beef chop
churros	fried pastry cut into lengths
cigalas	crayfish
cigalas cocidas	boiled crayfish
ciruelas	plums
ciruelas pasas	prunes
cochinillo asado	roast sucking pig
cocido	stew made with meat, chickpeas, vegetables etc.
cocktail de bogavante	lobster cocktail
cocochas (de merluza)	hake stew
cóctel de gambas	prawn cocktail
cóctel de langostinos	king prawn cocktail
cóctel de mariscos	seafood cocktail

codornices	quail
codornices asadas	roasted quail
codornices con uvas	quail cooked with grapes
codornices escabechadas	marinated quail
codornices estofadas	braised quail
col	cabbage
coles de Bruselas	Brussels sprouts
coles de Bruselas salteadas	sauté Brussels sprouts
coliflor	cauliflower
coliflor con bechamel	cauliflower with béchamel sauce and cheese
coñac	brandy
conejo asado	roast rabbit
conejo encebollado	rabbit served with onions
conejo estofado	braised rabbit
congrio	conger eel
consomé al jerez	consommé with sherry
consomé con yema	consommé with egg yolk
consomé de ave	chicken consommé
consomé de pollo	chicken consommé
contra de ternera con guisantes	veal stew with peas
contrafilete de ternera	veal fillet
copa...	... cup
copa de helado	ice cream, assorted flavours
cordero asado	roast lamb
cordero chilindrón	lamb stew with onion, tomato, peppers and eggs
costillas de cerdo	pork ribs
crema catalana	crème brûlée
crema de cangrejos	cream of crab soup
crema de espárragos	cream of asparagus soup
crema de legumbres	cream of vegetable soup
cremada	sweet made with egg, sugar and milk
crepe imperial	crêpe suzette
criadillas de tierra	ground tubers
crocante	ice cream with chopped nuts
croquetas	croquettes
croquetas de jamón	ham croquettes
croquetas de pescado	fish croquettes
cuajada	curds
dátiles	dates
embutidos	sausages

embutidos de la tierra	local sausages
embutidos variados	assorted sausages
empanada gallega	fish pie
empanada santiaguesa	fish pie
empanadillas de bonito	small tuna pies
empanadillas de carne	meat pies
empanadillas de chorizo	Spanish sausage pie
endivias	endives
ensaimada mallorquina	cake
ensalada de arenque	fish salad
ensalada de atún	tuna salad
ensalada de frutas	fruit salad
ensalada de gambas	prawn salad
ensalada de lechuga	lettuce salad
ensalada de pollo	chicken salad
ensalada de tomate	tomato salad
ensalada ilustrada	mixed salad
ensalada mixta	mixed salad
ensalada simple	green salad
ensaladilla	Spanish salad
ensaladilla rusa	Russian salad
entrecot a la parrilla	grilled entrecôte
entrecot de ternera	veal entrecôte
entremeses de la casa	hors d'œuvres
entremeses variados	hors d'œuvres
escalope a la milanesa	breaded veal with cheese
escalope a la parrilla	grilled veal
escalope a la plancha	grilled veal
escalope de lomo de cerdo	escalope of fillet of pork
escalope de ternera	veal escalope
escalope empanado	breaded escalope
escalopines al vino de Marsala	(veal) escalopes cooked in wine
escalopines de ternera	escalopes
escarola	lettuce *(crinkly)*
espadín a la toledana	kebab
espaguetis italiana	spaghetti
espárragos	asparagus
espárragos con mayonesa (*or* mahonesa)	asparagus with mayonnaise
espinacas	spinach
espinacas a la crema	spinach à la crème
espinazo de cerdo con patatas	pork ribs with potatoes *(stew)*

estofado de...	... stew
estofado de liebre	hare stew
estofados	stews
fabada (asturiana)	bean stew with sausage
faisán con castañas	pheasant with chestnuts
faisán estofado	stewed pheasant
faisán trufado	pheasant with truffles
fiambres	cold meats
fideos	thin pasta, noodles
filete a la parrilla	grilled beef
filete de cerdo	pork steak
filete de ternera	veal steak
flan	cream caramel
flan al ron	cream caramel with rum
flan de caramelo	cream caramel
fresas con nata	strawberries with cream
fruta	fruit
fruta variada	assorted fresh fruit
frutas en almíbar	fruit with syrup
gallina en pepitoria	chicken stewed with peppers
gambas a la americana	prawns
gambas a la plancha	grilled prawns
gambas al ajillo	prawns with garlic
gambas cocidas	boiled prawns
gambas con mayonesa	prawns with mayonnaise
gambas en gabardina	prawns in batter
gambas rebozadas	prawns in batter
garbanzos	chickpeas
garbanzos a la catalana	chickpeas with sausage, boiled eggs and pine seeds
gazpacho andaluz	cold tomato soup
gelatina de...	... gelatine
gratén de...	... au gratin
guisantes con jamón	peas with ham
guisantes salteados	sauté peas
habas	broad beans
habas con jamón	broad beans with ham
habas fritas	fried young broad beans
habichuelas	beans
helado de caramelo	caramel ice cream
helado de chocolate	chocolate ice cream
helado de fresa	strawberry ice cream

helado de mantecado	vanilla ice cream
helado de nata	plain ice cream
helado de vainilla	vanilla ice cream
hígado	liver
hígado con cebolla	liver cooked with onion
hígado de ternera estofado	liver of veal *(braised)*
hígado estofado	braised liver
higos con miel y nueces	figs with honey and nuts
higos secos	dried figs
horchata (de chufas)	cold almond-flavoured milk drink
huevo hilado	egg yolk garnish
huevos	eggs
huevos a la flamenca	fried eggs with ham, tomato and vegetables
huevos cocidos	hard boiled eggs
huevos con jamón	eggs with ham
huevos con mayonesa	boiled eggs with mayonnaise
huevos con panceta	eggs with bacon
huevos con patatas fritas	fried eggs and chips
huevos con picadillo	eggs with minced sausage
huevos con salchichas	eggs and sausages
huevos escalfados	poached eggs
huevos fritos	fried eggs
huevos fritos con chorizo	fried eggs with Spanish sausage
huevos fritos con jamón	fried eggs with ham
huevos pasados por agua	soft-boiled eggs
huevos rellenos	stuffed eggs
huevos revueltos con tomate	scrambled eggs with tomato
jamón con huevo hilado	ham with egg yolk garnish
jamón de Jabugo	Spanish ham
jamón de Trevélez	Spanish ham
jamón serrano	cured ham
jarra de vino	wine jug
jerez amontillado	pale dry sherry
jerez fino	pale, light sherry
jerez oloroso	sweet sherry
jeta	pork cheeks
judías verdes	French beans
judías verdes a la española	bean stew
judías verdes al natural	plain French beans
judías verdes con jamón	French beans with ham
jugo de albaricoque	apricot juice

jugo de lima	lime juice
jugo de limón	lemon juice
jugo de melocotón	peach juice
jugo de naranja	orange juice
jugo de piña	pineapple juice
jugo de tomate	tomato juice
Jumilla	light red and white "mistela" wines
langosta a la americana	lobster with brandy and garlic
langosta a la catalana	lobster with mushrooms and ham in a béchamel sauce
langosta fría con mayonesa	cold lobster with mayonnaise
langosta gratinada	lobster au gratin
langostinos a la plancha	grilled king prawns
langostinos con mayonesa	king prawns with mayonnaise
langostinos dos salsas	king prawns cooked in two sauces
leche frita	pudding with milk and eggs
leche merengada	cold milk with meringues
lechuga	lettuce
lengua de buey	ox tongue
lengua de cordero estofada	stewed lamb tongue
lenguado a la parrilla	grilled sole
lenguado a la plancha	grilled sole
lenguado a la romana	battered sole
lenguado frito	fried sole
lenguado grillado	grilled sole
lenguado meuniere	sole meunière
lentejas	lentils
lentejas aliñadas	lentils with vinaigrette
licores	spirits, liqueurs
liebre estofada	stewed hare
lombarda rellena	stuffed red cabbage
lombarda salteada	sauté red cabbage
lomo curado	pork sausage
lonchas de jamón	cured ham (sliced)
lubina a la marinera	sea bass in a parsley sauce
lubina al horno	baked sea bass
macarrones	macaroni
macarrones gratinados	macaroni cheese
macedonia de fruta	fruit salad
Málaga	sweet wine
mandarinas	tangerines
manises	peanuts

manitas de cordero	shank of lamb
manos de cerdo	pigs' trotters
manos de cerdo a la parrilla	grilled pigs' trotters
mantecadas	small sponge cakes
matequilla	butter
manzanas	apples
manzanas asadas	baked apples
manzanilla	dry sherry-type wine
mariscada	cold mixed shellfish
mariscos del día	fresh shellfish
mariscos del tiempo	seasonal shellfish
mazapán	marzipan
medallones de anguila	eel steaks
medallones de merluza	hake steaks
media de agua	half-bottle of mineral water
mejillones	mussels
mejillones a la marinera	mussels in a wine sauce
melocotón	peach
melocotones en almíbar	peaches in syrup
melón	melon
melón con jamón	melon with ham
membrillo	quince jelly
menestra de legumbres	vegetable stew
menú de la casa	fixed price menu
menú del día	set menu
merluza a la cazuela	stewed hake
merluza a la parrilla	grilled hake
merluza a la plancha	grilled hake
merluza a la riojana	hake with chilis
merluza a la romana	hake steaks in batter
merluza a la vasca	hake in a garlic sauce
merluza al ajo arriero	hake with garlic and chilis
merluza en salsa	hake in sauce
merluza en salsa verde	hake in a parsley and wine sauce
merluza fría	cold hake
merluza frita	fried hake
mermelada	jam
mermelada de albaricoque	apricot jam
mermelada de ciruelas	prune jam
mermelada de frambuesas	raspberry jam
mermelada de fresas	strawberry jam
mermelada de limón	lemon marmalade

mermelada de melocotón	peach jam
mermelada de naranja	marmalade
mero	grouper *(fish)*
mero a la parrilla	grilled grouper
mero en salsa verde	grouper with garlic and parsley sauce
mollejas de ternera fritas	fried sweetbreads
morcilla	black pudding
morcilla de carnero	black pudding made from mutton
morros de cerdo	pigs' cheeks
morros de vaca	cheeks of beef
morteruelo	kind of mince pie
mousse de...	... mousse
mousse de chocolate	chocolate mousse
mousse de limón	lemon mousse
nabo	turnip
naranjas	oranges
natillas	cold custard
natillas de chocolate	cold custard with chocolate
níscalos	wild mushrooms
nísperos	Sharon fruit
nueces	walnuts
orejas de cerdo	pigs' ears
otros mariscos según precios en plaza	other shellfish depending on current prices
paella	fried rice with various seafoods and chicken
paella castellana	fried rice with meat
paella de marisco	fried rice with shellfish
paella de pollo	fried rice with chicken
paella valenciana	fried rice with various shellfish and chicken
paleta de cordero lechal	shoulder of lamb
pan	bread
pan de higos	dried fig cake with cinnamon
panache de verduras	vegetable stew
panceta	bacon
parrillada de caza	mixed grilled game
parrillada de mariscos	mixed grilled shellfish
pasas	raisins
pastel de...	... cake
pastel de ternera	veal pie
pasteles	cakes

patatas a la pescadora	potatoes with fish
patatas asadas	roast potatoes
patatas bravas	potatoes in cayenne sauce
patatas fritas	chips, crisps
patitos rellenos	stuffed duckling
pato a la naranja	duck à l'orange
pato asado	roast duck
pato estofado	stewed duck
pavipollo	large chicken
pavo asado	roast turkey
pavo relleno	stuffed turkey
pavo trufado	turkey stuffed with truffles
pecho de ternera	breast of veal
pechuga de pollo	breast of chicken
pepinillos	gherkins
pepinillos en vinagreta	gherkins in vinaigrette sauce
pepino	cucumber
peras	pears
percebes	shellfish (edible barnacle)
perdices a la campesina	partridges with vegetables
perdices a la manchega	partridges in red wine with garlic, herbs and pepper
perdices asadas	roast partridges
perdices con chocolate	partridges with chocolate
perdices escabechadas	marinated partridges
perejil	parsley
pescaditos fritos	fried fish
pestiños	sugared pastries with anis
pez espada ahumado	smoked swordfish
picadillo de ternera	minced veal
pimientos a la riojana	baked red peppers fried in oil and garlic
pimientos fritos	fried peppers
pimientos morrones	strong peppers
pimientos rellenos	stuffed peppers
pimientos verdes	green peppers
piña al gratín	pineapple au gratin
piña fresca	fresh pineapple
pinchitos	snacks served in bars
pinchos	snacks served in bars
pinchos morunos	kebabs
piñones	pine seeds

pisto	fried mixed vegetables
pisto manchego	marrow with onion and tomato
plátanos	bananas
plátanos flameados	bananas flambé
pollo a la parrilla	grilled chicken
pollo a la riojana	chicken with peppers and chilis
pollo al ajillo	fried chicken with garlic
pollo al champaña	chicken au champagne
pollo al vino blanco	chicken in white wine
pollo asado	roast chicken
pollo braseado	braised chicken
pollo con tomate	chicken with tomatoes
pollo con verduras	chicken and vegetables
pollo en cacerola	chicken casserole
pollo en pepitoria	chicken in wine with saffron, garlic and almonds
pollo salteado	chicken sauté
pollos tomateros con zanhorias	young chicken with carrots
polvorones	sugar-based sweet *(eaten at Christmas)*
pomelo	grapefruit
potaje castellano	thick broth
potaje de garbanzos	chickpea stew
potaje de habichuelas	white bean stew
potaje de lentejas	lentil stew
puchero canario	casserole containing meat, chickpeas and corn
pulpitos con cebolla	baby octopus with onions
pulpo	octopus
puré de patatas	potato puré
purrusalda	cod with leeks and potatoes
queso con membrillo	cheese with quince jelly
queso de Burgos	soft white cheese
queso de bola	Dutch cheese
queso de oveja	sheep's cheese
queso del país	local cheese
queso gallego	creamy cheese
queso manchego	hard strong cheese
quisquillas	shrimps
rábanos	radish
ragout de ternera	veal ragout
rape a la americana	white fish with brandy and herbs
rape a la cazuela	stewed white fish

rape a la plancha	grilled white fish
raviolis	ravioli
raya	skate
redondo al horno	roast fillet of beef
remolacha	beetroot
repollo	cabbage
repostería de la casa	cakes baked on the premises
requesón	cream cheese/cottage cheese
revuelto de ajos tiernos	scrambled eggs with spring garlic
revuelto de angulas	scrambled eggs with baby eels
revuelto de gambas	scrambled eggs with prawns
revuelto de sesos	scrambled eggs with brains
revuelto de trigueros	scrambled eggs with asparagus
revuelto mixto	scrambled eggs with mixed vegetables
Ribeiro	white wines
riñones	kidneys
riñones al jerez	kidneys with sherry
Rioja	the finest wines in Spain
rodaballo	turbot
romero	tarragon
ron	rum
roscas	sweet pastries
salchichas	sausages
salchichas de Frankfurt	Frankfurter sausages
salchichón	white sausage with pepper
salmón a la parrilla	grilled salmon
salmón ahumado	smoked salmon
salmón frío	cold salmon
salmonetes	red mullet
salmonetes a la parrilla	grilled red mullet
salmonetes en papillote	red mullet cooked in foil
salmorejo	marinated fish
salpicón de mariscos	shellfish with vinaigrette
salsa allioli *or* **ali oli**	mayonnaise with garlic
salsa bechamel	white sauce
salsa de tomate	tomato sauce
salsa holandesa	hot sauce made with eggs and butter
salsa mahonesa *or* **mayonesa**	mayonnaise
salsa tártara	tartare sauce
salsa vinagreta	vinaigrette sauce
sandía	water melon

sangría	mixture of red wine, lemonade, spirits and fruit
sardinas a la brasa	barbecued sardines
sardinas a la parrilla	grilled sardines
sardinas fritas	fried sardines
seco	dry
semidulce	medium sweet
sesos a la romana	fried brains in batter
sesos rebozados	brains in batter
setas a la plancha	grilled mushrooms
setas rellenas	stuffed mushrooms
sidra	cider
solomillo con guisantes	fillet steak with peas
solomillo con patatas	fillet steak with potatoes
solomillo de ternera	fillet of veal
solomillo de vaca	fillet of beef
solomillo frío	cold roast beef
sopa	soup
sopa castellana	vegetable soup
sopa de ajo	garlic soup
sopa de almendras	almond-based pudding
sopa de cola de buey	oxtail soup
sopa de fideos	noodle soup
sopa de gallina	chicken soup
sopa de legumbres	vegetable soup
sopa de lentejas	lentil soup
sopa de marisco	fish and shellfish soup
sopa de pescado	fish soup
sopa de rabo de buey	oxtail soup
sopa de verduras	vegetable soup
sopa del día	soup of the day
sopa mallorquina	soup with tomato, meat and eggs
sopa sevillana	fish and mayonnaise soup
sorbete	sorbet
soufflé	soufflé
soufflé de fresones	strawberry soufflé
soufflé de naranja	orange soufflé
soufflé de queso	cheese soufflé
suplemento de verduras	extra vegetables
tallarines	noodles
tallarines a la italiana	tagliatelle
tarta de almendra	almond tart

tarta de chocolate	chocolate tart
tarta de fresas	strawberry tart
tarta de la casa	tart baked on the premises
tarta de manzana	apple tart
tarta helada	ice cream gateau
tarta moca	mocha tart
tencas	tench
ternera asada	roast veal
tocinillos de cielo	crème caramel
tomates rellenos	stuffed tomatoes
tordo	thrush
torrijas	sweet pastries
tortilla Alaska	baked Alaska
tortilla a la paisana	omelette containing different vegetables
tortilla a su gusto	omelette made to the customer's wishes
tortilla de bonito	tuna fish omelette
tortilla de champiñones	mushroom omelette
tortilla de chorizo	omelette containing spiced sausage
tortilla de escabeche	fish omelette
tortilla de espárragos	asparagus omelette
tortilla de gambas	prawn omelette
tortilla de jamón	ham omelette
tortilla de patatas	potato omelette
tortilla de sesos	brain omelette
tortilla de setas	mushroom omelette
tortilla española	potato omelette
tortilla sacromonte	vegetable, brains and sausage omelette
tortillas variadas	various omelettes
tournedó	tournedos *(fillet steak)*
trucha ahumada	smoked trout
trucha con jamón	trout with ham
trucha escabechada	marinated trout
truchas a la marinera	trout in wine sauce
truchas molinera	trout meunière
trufas	truffles
turrón	nougat
turrón de Alicante	hard nougat
turrón de Jijona	soft nougat
turrón de coco	coconut nougat

turrón de yema	nougat with egg yolk
uvas	grapes
Valdepeñas	fruity red wines
vieiras	scallops
vino blanco	white wine
vino de mesa	table wine
vino rosado	rosé wine
vino tinto	red wine
zanahorias a la crema	carrots à la crème
zarzuela de mariscos	seafood stew
zarzuela de pescados y mariscos	fish and shellfish stew
zumo de...	... juice
zumo de albaricoque	apricot juice
zumo de lima	lime juice
zumo de limón	lemon juice
zumo de melocotón	peach juice
zumo de naranja	orange juice
zumo de piña	pineapple juice
zumo de tomate	tomato juice

SHOPPING

The latest changes in the law allow shops to stay open as they wish, but most stick to the usual hours of 9 am – 1.30 pm and 4.30 pm to 7.30 pm. In summer a longer lunch break means that shops stay open in the afternoon from 5 – 8.30 pm approx. Most shops close at 2 pm on Saturdays. Large department stores do not close for lunch and are open longer on Saturdays.

See the Health section for details about chemists; toiletries and non-drug items can be bought from supermarkets and department stores (or from a *Perfumería*, where they'll probably cost a bit more).

USEFUL WORDS AND PHRASES

audio equipment	aparatos de música	*aparah-toss deh moossika*
baker	la panadería	*pannadeh-ree-a*
bookshop	la librería	*leebreh-reea*
boutique	la boutique	*booteek*
butcher	la carnicería	*carnee-theh-ree-a*
bookshop	la librería	*leebreh-ree-a*
to buy	comprar	*komprar*
cake shop	la pastelería	*pasteh-leh-ree-a*
cheap	barato	*barah-toh*
chemist	la farmacia	*farmath-ya*
department store	los grandes almacenes	*grandess almatheh-ness*
fashion	la moda	*moh-da*
fishmonger	la pescadería	*pesskadeh-ree-a*
florist	la floristería	*floreess-teh-ree-a*
grocer	la tienda de comestibles	*tee-enda deh comesstee-bless*
ironmonger	la ferretería	*ferreh-teh-ree-a*
ladies' wear	señoras	*sen-yorass*
menswear	caballeros	*kabayeh-ross*

newsagent	el kiosko de periódicos	*kee-oskoh deh peree-oddee-koss*
pharmacy	la farmacia	*farmath-ya*
receipt	la factura	*faktoora*
record shop	la tienda de discos	*tee-enda deh deeskoss*
sale	rebajas, liquidación	*rebah-Hass, leekee-dath-yon*
shoe shop	la zapatería	*thapateh-ree-a*
shop	la tienda	*tee-enda*
to go shopping	ir de compras	*eer deh komprass*
souvenir shop	la tienda de regalos	*tee-enda deh regah-loss*
special offer	una oferta	*offair-ta*
to spend	gastar	*gass-tar*
stationer	la papelería	*papeh-leh-ree-a*
supermarket	el supermercado	*sooper-mair-kah-doh*
tailor	la sastrería	*sasstreh-ree-a*
till	la caja	*kah-Ha*
toyshop	la juguetería	*Hoo-gheh-teh-ree-a*
travel agent	la agencia de viajes	*aHenth-ya deh vee-ah-Hess*

I'd like...
Querría...
keh-ree-a

Do you have...?
¿Tienen...?
tee-eh-nen

How much is this?
¿Cuánto es esto?
kwantoh ess esstoh

Do you have any more of these?
¿Tiene alguno más de éstos?
tee-eh-neh algoonoh mass deh esstoss

Have you anything cheaper?
¿Tiene usted algo más barato?
tee-eh-neh oosteh algoh mass barah-toh

Have you anything larger?
¿Tiene usted algo más grande?
tee-eh-neh oosteh algoh mass grandeh

Have you anything smaller?
¿Tiene usted algo más pequeño?
tee-eh-neh oosteh algoh mass peh-kain-yoh

Does it come in other colours?
¿Lo hay en otros colores?
loh I en oh-tross koloress

Can I try it (them) on?
¿Puedo probármelo(s)?
pweh-doh probarmeh-loh(oss)

I'd like to change this, please
Quería cambiar esto
keh-ree-a kambee-ar esstoh

Can I have a refund?
¿Pueden devolverme el dinero?
pweh-den deh-volvair-meh el deeneh-roh

Where is the ... department?
¿Dónde está la sección de...?
dondeh essta la sekth-yon deh

Could you wrap it for me?
¿Podría envolvérmelo?
podree-a embol-vairmeh-loh

Can I have a bag please?
¿Me da una bolsa, por favor?
meh da oona bolsa, por fa-vor

Where do I pay?
¿Dónde se paga?
dondeh seh pah-ga

Can I have a receipt?
¿Me da una factura?
meh da oona faktoora

I'm just looking
Sólo estoy mirando
soloh esstoy meerandoh

REPLIES YOU MAY BE GIVEN

¿Le están atendiendo?
Are you being served?

Por favor, use un carrito/una cesta
Please take a trolley/basket

Lo siento, se nos han terminado
I'm sorry, we're out of stock

Esto es todo lo que tenemos
This is all we have

No podemos devolver el importe
We cannot give cash refunds

¿No tiene más que eso?
Have you anything smaller?

THINGS YOU'LL SEE OR HEAR

agencia de viajes	travel agent
alimentación	groceries
alquiler	rental
autoservicio	self-service
barato	cheap
bricolage	Do-it-yourself supplies
caballeros	menswear
calidad	quality
calzados	shoe shop
carnicería	butcher
droguería	household cleaning materials
estanco	tobacconist
flores	flowers
ganga	bargain
grandes almacenes	department store
helados	ice-cream shop
juquetes	toys
librería	bookshop
moda	fashion
objetos de escritorio	office supplies
oferta	special offer
panadería	bakery
papelería	stationer
pastelería	cake shop
peletería	furrier
planta sótano	lower floor
planta superior	upper floor
precio	price
rebajado	reduced
rebajas de verano	summer sale
sección	department
señoras	ladies' department
verduras	vegetables

AT THE HAIRDRESSER

The hairdressing shop is called a *peluquería*. A men's hairdresser is more usually *la barbería* – easily recognised by the traditional barber's pole or a similar device with red, white and blue stripes.

USEFUL WORDS AND PHRASES

appointment	hora	*ora*
beard	la barba	*barba*
blond	rubio	*roob-yoh*
brush	el cepillo	*thepee-yoh*
comb	el peine	*pay-neh*
conditioner	la crema acondicionadora	*kreh-ma akondeeth-yona-dora*
curlers	los rulos	*rooloss*
curling tongs	las pinzas eléctricas	*peenthass elektrikass*
curly	rizado	*reethah-doh*
dark	oscuro	*osskooroh*
fringe	el flequillo	*flekee-yoh*
gel	un gel	*Hell*
hair	el pelo	*peh-loh*
haircut	un corte	*korteh*
hairdresser	el peluquero/ la peluquera	*pelookeh-roh pelookeh-ra*
hairdryer	el secador	*seh-kador*
highlights	reflejos	*refleh-Hoss*
long	largo	*largoh*
moustache	el bigote	*beegoh-teh*
parting	la raya	*rayya*
perm	una permanente	*pairma-nenteh*
shampoo	un lavado	*lavah-doh*
shave	afeitar	*affay-tar*
shaving foam	la espuma de afeitar	*esspooma deh affay-tar*

short	corto	*kortoh*
styling mousse	la espuma moldeadora	*esspooma moldeh-adora*
wavy	ondulado	*ondoolah-doh*

I'd like to make an appointment
Quería pedir hora
keh-ree-a pedeer ora

Just a trim please
Recórtemelo un poco solamente, por favor
rekorteh-meh-loh oon pokoh sola-menteh, por fa-vor

Not too much off
No me corte demasiado
noh meh korteh demass-yah-doh

A bit more off here please
Córtemelo un poco más por aquí, por favor
korteh-meh-loh oon pokoh mass por akee, por fa-vor

I'd like a cut and blow-dry
Quería un corte y moldeado con secador de mano
keh-ree-a oon korteh ee moldeh-ah-doh kon sekador deh mah-noh

I'd like a perm
Quería una permanente
keh-ree-a oona pairma-nenteh

I'd like highlights
Quería mechas
keh-ree-a may-chas

THINGS YOU'LL SEE OR HEAR

afeitado	shave
barbería	barber
lavado	wash
lavado y marcado	wash and set
marcado	set
moldeado con secador de mano	blow-dry
peluquería de caballeros	men's hairdresser
peluquería de señoras	ladies' salon
peluquero/peluquera	hair stylist, hairdresser
permanente	perm
salón de peluquería	hairdressing salon
seco	dry
tinte	tint

SPORTS

Thanks to Spain's excellent climate almost all outdoor sports are well catered for. The east and south coasts especially provide excellent opportunites for swimming, water-skiing, sailing, fishing (including underwater) and sailboarding. The north coast also has good facilities but is less popular due to the cooler climate. A flag warning system operates on most beaches: red for dangerous conditions, yellow for caution and green for all clear. Hiring equipment poses no problem and everything from a parasol to a sailboard is covered at a reasonable charge. Golf, which has become very popular, offers play all the year round and courses exist in Madrid and nearly all the major beach resorts. Tennis courts can be found in most places and squash is gaining in popularity. In areas such as the Pyrenees and Sierra Nevada there is ample scope for walking, mountaineering, and skiing in the winter.

USEFUL WORDS AND PHRASES

athletics	el atletismo	*atleh-teezmoh*
badminton	el badminton	*badmeen-tonn*
ball	la pelota	*peh-loh-ta*
beach	la playa	*playya*
bicycle	una bicicleta	*beethee-kleh-ta*
canoe	una piragua	*peerah-gwa*
canoeing	el piragüismo	*peerag-weezmoh*
deckchair	una tumbona	*toomboh-na*
diving board	un trampolin	*trampoh-leen*
fins	las aletas	*aleh-tass*
fishing	la pesca	*pesska*
fishing rod	una caña de pescar	*kahn-ya deh pesskar*
football	el balón	*ba-lon*
football match	un partido de fútbol	*partee-doh deh foot-bol*
goggles	las gafas de bucear	*gah-fass deh bootheh-ar*

75

golf	el golf	
golf course	un campo de golf	_kampoh deh golf_
gymnastics	la gimnasia	_Heemnass-ya_
harpoon	el fusil submarino	_foo-seel soobma-reenoh_
hockey	el hockey	_Hokkay_
jogging	el footing	_footeen_
lake	un lago	_lah-goh_
mountaineering	el montañismo	_montan-yeezmoh_
oxygen bottles	las botellas de oxígeno	_botell-yass deh oksee-Hennoh_
pedal boat	un hidropedal	_eedroh-peh-dal_
racket	una raqueta	_rakeh-ta_
riding	la equitación	_ekeetath-yon_
rowing boat	una barca de remos	_barka deh reh-moss_
to run	correr	_kor-air_
sailboard	una tabla de windsurfing	_tah-bla deh weendsoorfeen_
sailing	(hacer) vela	_(athair) veh-la_
sand	la arena	_arreh-na_
sea	el mar	_mar_
to skate	patinar	_pateenar_
skates	los patines	_patee-ness_
skin diving	el submarinismo	_soobmaree-neezmoh_
snorkel	el respirador	_resspeera-dor_
stadium	el estadio	_esstahd-yoh_
sunshade	una sombrilla	_sombree-ya_
to swim	nadar	_nadar_
swimming pool	la piscina	_peessthee-na_
tennis	el tenis	_teh-neess_
tennis court	una pista de tenis	_peessta deh teh-neess_
tennis racket	una raqueta de tenis	_rakeh-ta deh teh-neess_
tent	una tienda (de campaña)	_tee-enda (deh kampahn-ya)_
underwater fishing	la pesca submarina	_pesska soobmaree-na_
volleyball	el voléibol	_vollay-bol_
walking	andar	_andar_
water skiing	el esquí acuático	_esskee akwatee-koh_

water skis	los esquís acuáticos	*esskeess akwatee-koss*
wave	una ola	*oh-la*
wet suit	un traje isotérmico	*trah-Heh eessoh -tairmee-koh*
yacht	un yate	*yah-teh*

How do I get to the beach?
¿Por dónde se va a la playa?
por dondeh seh va ah la pla-ya

How deep is the water here?
¿Qué profundidad tiene el agua aquí?
keh profoondee-da tee-eh-neh el ah-gwa akee

Is there an indoor/outdoor pool here?
¿Hay piscina cubierta/al aire libre aquí?
I peessthee-na koob-yairta/al I-reh leebreh akee

Is it safe to swim here?
¿Se puede nadar sin peligro aquí?
seh pweh-deh nadar seen pelee-groh akee

Can I fish here?
¿Puedo pescar aquí?
pweh-doh pesskar akee

Do I need a licence?
¿Necesito un permiso?
nethessee-toh oon pair-meessoh

I would like to hire a sunshade
Quería alquilar una sombrilla
keh-ree-a alkee-lar oona sombree-ya

How much does it cost per hour/day?
¿Cuánto cuesta por hora/por día?
kwantoh kwessta por ora/ por dee-a

77

I would like to take water-skiing lessons
Quería dar clases de esquí acuático
keh-ree-a dar klah-sess deh esskee akwatee-koh

Where can I hire...?
¿Dónde puedo alquilar...?
dondeh pweh-doh alkee-lar

THINGS YOU'LL SEE OR HEAR

alquiler de barcos	boat hire
alquiler de esquís	water-ski hire
alquiler de sombrillas	sunshade hire
alquiler de tablas	board hire
bucear	to go diving
campo de golf	golf course
corriente peligrosa	dangerous current
hacer vela	to sail
hacer windsurfing	to windsurf
montar a caballo	to go (horse) riding
nadar	to swim
palo de golf	golf-club
peatones	pedestrians
peligro	danger
piscina	swimming pool
piscina cubierta	indoor swimming pool
pista de tenis	tennis court
primeros auxilios	first aid
prohibido acampar	no camping
prohibido bañarse	no swimming
prohibido pescar	no fishing
remar	to row
socorrista	lifeguard
submarinismo	skin-diving
tomar el sol	to sunbathe

POST OFFICE

Post Offices in Spain deal only with mail and telegrams, so don't look for a phone there; use a call box or find the exchange *(Telefónica)*. Stamps can be bought in the post office but most Spaniards go to an *estanco* (a state tobacconist shop – look for the red and yellow sign) where you can also buy postcards. Letter boxes are yellow.

USEFUL WORDS AND PHRASES

airmail	correo aéreo	*korreh-oh ah-aireh-oh*
collection	la recogida	*reh-koh-Heeda*
counter	el mostrador	*mostra-dor*
customs form	el impreso para la aduana	*eempreh-soh parra la adwah-na*
delivery	el reparto	*reh-partoh*
deposit	un depósito	*deh-pozzitoh*
form	un impreso	*eempreh-soh*
letter	una carta	*karta*
letter box	el buzón	*boothon*
mail	el correo	*korreh-oh*
money order	un giro (postal)	*Hee-roh (posstal)*
package/parcel	un paquete	*pakeh-teh*
post	el correo	*korreh-oh*
postage rates	las tarifas postales	*tarree-fass posstah-less*
postal order	un giro postal	*Hee-roh posstal*
postcard	una postal	*posstal*
postcode	el distrito postal	*deesstree-toh posstal*
poste-restante	la lista de correos	*leessta deh korreh-oss*
postman	el cartero	*karteh-roh*
post office	(la oficina de) correos	*(offee-theena deh) korreh-oss*
registered letter	una carta certificada	*karta thair-teefee-kah-da*
savings	los ahorros	*ah-orross*

stamp	un sello	*seyyoh*
surface mail	correo ordinario	*korreh-oh ordee-nar-yoh*
telegram	un telegrama	*telleh-grah-ma*

How much is a letter/postcard to...?
¿Qué franqueo lleva una carta/una postal a...?
keh fran-keh-oh yeh-va oona karta/oona posstal ah

I would like three 35 peseta stamps
Quería tres sellos de treinta y cinco pesetas
keh-ree-a tress seyyoss deh train-ta ee theenkoh peh-seh-tass

I want to register this letter
Quiero mandar esta carta certificada
kee-eh-roh mandar essta karta thair-teefee-kah-da

I want to send this parcel to...
Quiero mandar este paquete a...
kee-eh-roh mandar essteh pakeh-teh ah

How long does the post (mail) to ... take?
¿Cuánto tarda el correo para...?
kwantoh tarda el korreh-oh parra

Where can I post (mail) this?
¿Dónde puedo echar esto?
dondeh pweh-doh etchar esstoh

Is there any mail for me?
¿Hay algún correo para mí?
I algoon korreh-oh parra mee

I'd like to send a telegram
Quería poner un telegrama
keh-ree-a ponnair oon teleh-grah-ma

This is to go airmail
Esto quiero que vaya por avión
esstoh kee-eh-roh keh vayya por av-yon

THINGS YOU'LL SEE OR HEAR

buzón	letterbox
carta	letter
certificados	registered mail
correo aéreo	airmail
correo urgente	express
correos	post office
destinatario	addressee
dirección	address
distrito postal	post code
España	inland postage
extranjero	postage abroad
franqueo	postage
giros	money orders
horas de oficina	opening hours
horas de recogida	collection times
lista de correos	poste-restante
localidad	place
paquete	packet
paquetes	parcels counter
postal	postcard
rellenar	to fill in
remitente	sender
sello	stamp
tarifa	charge
telegramas	telegrams
venta de sellos	stamps

TELEPHONE

Telephone boxes in Spain are metallic-grey and have the words URBANA – INTERURBANA –INTERNACIONAL written on a green panel at the top. To call the UK or USA from an *Internacional* kiosk, dial 07 and wait for a high-pitched tone, then dial 44 (for UK) or 1 (USA) followed by the area code and the number you want. Remember to omit the 0 which prefixes all UK area codes.

The tones you hear on Spanish phones differ slightly from ours:
Dialling tone: same as in UK or USA
Ringing : repeated long tone
Engaged : rapid pips

For international calls first insert a 50 peseta coin in the slot and then use smaller coins of 25 ptas to prolong the call. For local calls use 5 ptas coins, and for long-distance use 25 ptas.

There are also pay-phones in bars and restaurants, where you may still have to buy a token *(ficha)* to use instead of a coin. Alternatively you can look for the *Central Telefónica* or *Teléfonos*. Run by CTNE (look for the initials, standing for Spain's national telephone company), these are often open 24 hours a day in major towns. You ask at the cash desk for the number you want, go to a booth and wait for it to be obtained for you, and pay when you have finished your call.

USEFUL WORDS AND PHRASES

call	una llamada	*yamah-da*
to call	llamar	*yamar*
code	el prefijo	*preh-fee-Hoh*
crossed line	un cruce de líneas	*krootheh deh leeneh-ass*
to dial	marcar	*markar*
dialling tone	la señal para marcar	*sen-yal parra markar*
emergency	una emergencia	*emmair-Henth-ya*
enquiries	información	*eenformath-yon*
extension	extensión	*ekstenth-yon*

international call	una llamada internacional	*yamah-da eentair-naīh-yonal*
number	el número	*noomeh-roh*
operator	la operadora	*opeh-radora*
pay-phone	un teléfono público	*teh-leffonoh pooblikoh*
push-button phone	un teléfono automático	*teh-leffonoh owtoh-matikoh*
receiver	el aparato	*aparah-toh*
reverse charge call	una llamada a cobro revertido	*yamah-da ah kobroh reh-vair-teedoh*
telephone	un teléfono	*teh-leffonoh*
telephone box	una cabina telefónica	*kabeena teleh-fonnika*
telephone directory	la guía telefónica	*ghee-a teleh-fonnika*
wrong number	el número equivocado	*noomeh-roh eh-keevoh-kah-doh*

Where is the nearest phone box?
¿Dónde está la cabina de teléfonos más cercana?
dondeh essta la kabeena deh teh-leffonoss mass thair-kah-na

Hello, this is ... speaking
Hola, soy...
oh-la, soy

Is that...?
¿Es (usted)...?
ess (oosteh)

Speaking
Al habla
al abla

I would like to speak to...
Quería hablar con...
keh-ree-a ablar kon

83

Extension ... please
Extensión ... por favor
ekstenss-yon ... por fa-vor

Please tell him ... called
Haga el favor de decirle que ha llamado...
ah-ga el fa-vor deh deh-theerleh keh ah yamah-doh

Ask him to call me back please
Digale que me llame cuando vuelva
dee-gah-leh keh meh yah-meh kwandoh vwelva

My number is...
Mi teléfono es el...
mee teh-leffonoh ess el

Do you know where he is?
¿Sabe usted dónde está?
sah-beh oosteh dondeh essta

When will he be back?
¿Cuándo volverá?
kwandoh volveh-ra

Could you leave him a message?
¿Podría dejarle un recado?
podree-a deh-Harleh oon reh-kah-doh

I'll ring back later
Volveré a llamar luego
volveh-reh a yamar lweh-goh

Sorry, wrong number
Perdone, me he equivocado de número
pairdoh-neh, meh eh eh-keevoh-kah-doh deh noomeh-roh

REPLIES YOU MAY BE GIVEN

¿Con quién quiere que le ponga?
Who would you like to speak to?

¿Cuál es su teléfono?
What is your number?

Lo siento, no está
Sorry, he's not in

Puede dejar un recado
You can leave a message

Volverá dentro de ... minutos/horas
He'll be back in ... minutes/hours

Vuelva llamar mañana, por favor
Please call again tomorrow

Le diré que le llame
I'll tell him you called

Is there a telephone directory?
¿Hay una guía de teléfonos?
I oona ghee-a deh teh-leffonoss

I would like the directory for...
Quería la guía telefonica de...
keh-ree-a la ghee-a teleh-fonnika deh

Can I call abroad from here?
¿Puedo llamar al extranjero desde aquí?
pweh-doh yamar al estran-Heh-roh dezdeh akee

How much is a call to...?
¿Cuánto cuesta una llamada a...?
kwantoh kwessta oona yamah-da ah

I would like to reverse the charges
Quiero que sea a cobro revertido
kee-eh-roh keh seh-ah ah kobroh reh-vair-teedoh

I would like a number in...
Quiero un número de...
kee-eh-roh oon noomeh-roh deh

Hello? (when answering)
Digame
dee-gah-meh

THINGS YOU'LL SEE OR HEAR

al aparato	speaking
bomberos	fire brigade
cabina telefónica	telephone box
central telefónica	telephone exchange
conferencia	call
conferencia internacional	international call
conferencia interurbana	long-distance call
conferencia urbana	local call
descolgar el aparato	lift receiver
¡dese prisa!	be brief!
diga/dígame	hello
fuego	fire
guía telefónica	telephone directory
insertar	to insert
llamada	call
lo siento, no está	sorry, he's not in
marcar	to dial
marque	dial
monedas	coins
no funciona	out of order
número	number
operadora	operator
páginas amarillas	yellow pages
paso (de contador)	unit
prefijo	code
reparaciones	faults service
servicio a través de operadora	dialling through the operator
servicio automático	direct dialling
tarifa	charges
teléfono	telephone

HEALTH

Under the EEC Social Security regulations visitors from the UK qualify for treatment on the same basis as the Spanish themselves. You must complete the form CM1 (at your own Social Security office) a month at least before travelling. You then get a certificate (E111) for use if you need treatment, plus an explanatory leaflet.

Medicines and drugs are available only from the *Farmacia* (chemists), usually open from 9am-1pm, 4pm-8pm. If shut, there'll be a notice on the door that gives the address of the 'duty chemist' *(Farmacias de Guardia)*. In case of sudden illness or accident, go to the nearest emergency first aid centre *(Casa de Socorro)* or – if on the road – *Puestos de Socorro*.

USEFUL WORDS AND PHRASES

accident	un accidente	akthee-denteh
ambulance	una ambulancia	amboolanth-ya
anaemic	anémico	anneh-mikoh
appendicitis	una apendicitis	apendee-theeteess
appendix	el apéndice	apen-deetheh
aspirin	una aspirina	asspee-reena
asthma	asma	azma
backache	un dolor de espalda	dolor deh esspalda
bandage	el vendaje	vendah-Heh
bite	una mordedura	mordeh-doora
(of insect)	una picadura	peeka-doora
bladder	la vejiga	veh-Heega
blister	una ampolla	ampoyya
blood	la sangre	sangreh
blood donor	un donante de sangre	doh-nanteh deh sangreh
burn	una quemadura	keh-madoora
cancer	cáncer	kanthair
chemist	la farmacia	farmath-ya

88

chest	el pecho	*petchoh*
chickenpox	la varicela	*varee-theh-la*
cold	un resfriado	*ressfree-ah-doh*
concussion	una conmoción	*konmoth-yon*
constipation	estreñimiento	*esstrain-yeem-yentoh*
contact lenses	las lentes de contacto	*lentess deh kontaktoh*
corn	un callo	*kayyoh*
cough	tos	*toss*
cut	una cortadura	*korta-doora*
dentist	el dentista	*denteessta*
diabetes	la diabetes	*dee-abeh-tess*
diarrhoea	una diarrea	*dee-arreh-a*
dizzy	mareado	*marreh-ah-doh*
doctor	el médico	*meddeekoh*
earache	un dolor de oídos	*dolor deh oh-eedoss*
fever	fiebre	*fee-eh-breh*
filling	un empaste	*empassteh*
first aid	primeros auxilios	*preemeh-ross owk-zeel-yoss*
flu	la gripe	*greepeh*
fracture	una fractura	*fraktoora*
German measles	la rubeola	*roobeh-ola*
glasses	las gafas	*gah-fass*
haemorrhage	una hemorragia	*emmoraH-ya*
hayfever	la fiebre del heno	*fee-eh-breh dell eh-noh*
headache	un dolor de cabeza	*dolor deh kabeh-tha*
heart	el corazón	*korrathon*
heart attack	un infarto	*eenfartoh*
hospital	el hospital	*osspeetal*
ill	enfermo	*emfairmoh*
indigestion	una indigestión	*eendee-Hest-yon*
injection	una inyección	*eenyekth-yon*
itch	un picor	*peekor*
kidney	el riñón	*reen-yon*
lump	un bulto	*booltoh*
measles	el sarampión	*saramp-yon*
migraine	una jaqueca	*Hakeh-ka*

mumps	las paperas	*papeh-rass*
nausea	náuseas	*now-seh-ass*
nurse	la enfermera	*emfairmeh-ra*
operation	una operación	*oppeh-rath-yon*
optician	el oculista	*okooleess-ta*
pain	un dolor	*dolor*
penicillin	la penicilina	*peneethee-leena*
plaster	la escayola	*esska-yola*
pneumonia	una neumonía	*neh-oomonee-a*
pregnant	embarazada	*embarra-thah-da*
prescription	una receta	*reh-theh-ta*
rheumatism	el reúma	*reh-oo-ma*
scald	una quemadura	*keh-madoora*
scratch	una arañazo	*arran-yah-thoh*
smallpox	la viruela	*veer-weh-la*
sore throat	un dolor de garganta	*dolor deh garganta*
splinter	una astilla	*assteel-ya*
sprain	una torcedura	*tortheh-doora*
sting	una picadura	*peeka-doora*
stomach	el estómago	*esstoh-magoh*
temperature	la temperatura	*tempeh-ratoora*
tonsils	las amígdalas	*ameegda-lass*
toothache	un dolor de muelas	*dolor deh mweh-lass*
travel sickness	mareo	*marreh-oh*
ulcer	una úlcera	*ooltheh-ra*
vaccination	la vacunación	*vakoonath-yon*
to vomit	vomitar	*vommee-tar*
whooping cough	la tosferina	*tossfeh-reena*

I have a pain in...
Me duele...
meh dweh-leh

I do not feel well
No me encuentro bien
noh meh enkwen-troh bee-en

I feel faint
Me encuentro débil
meh enkwen-troh deh-beel

I feel sick
Tengo náuseas
teng-goh now-seh-ass

I feel dizzy
Estoy mareado
esstoy marreh-ah-doh

It hurts here
Me duele aquí
meh dweh-leh akee

It's a sharp pain
Es un dolor agudo
ess oon dolor agoodoh

It's a dull pain
Es un dolor sordo
ess oon dolor sor-doh

It hurts all the time
Es un dolor continuo
ess oon dolor konteen-woh

It only hurts now and then
Sólo me duele a ratos
soloh meh dweh-leh ah rah-toss

It hurts when you touch it
Me duele al tocarlo
meh dweh-leh al tokarloh

It hurts more at night
Me duele más por la noche
meh dweh-leh mass por la notcheh

It stings
Me escuece
meh ess-kweh-theh

It aches
Me duele
meh dweh-leh

I have a temperature
Tengo fiebre
teng-go fee-eh-breh

I need a prescription for...
Necesito una receta para...
netheh-seetoh oona reh-theh-ta parra

I normally take...
Normalmente tomo...
normalmenteh toh-moh

I'm allergic to...
Soy alérgico a...
soy allair-Heekoh ah

Have you got anything for...?
¿Tiene usted algo para...?
tee-eh-neh oossteh algoh parra

Do I need a prescription for...?
¿Hace falta receta para...?
ah-theh falta reh-theh-ta parra

REPLIES YOU MAY BE GIVEN

Tome usted ... comprimidos/pastillas cada vez
Take ... pills/tablets at a time

Con agua
With water

Mastíquelos
Chew them

Una vez/dos veces/tres veces al día
Once/twice/three times a day

Al acostarse
Only when you go to bed

¿Qué toma normalmente?
What do you normally take?

Debería consultar a un médico
I think you should see a doctor

Lo siento, no lo tenemos
I'm sorry, we don't have that

Hace falta una receta médica para eso
For that you need a prescription

THINGS YOU'LL SEE OR HEAR

ambulancia	ambulance
Casa de Socorro	First Aid Post
clínica	clinic
consulta	surgery
dentista	dentist
empaste	filling
encía	gum
farmacia de guardia	duty chemist
flemón	abscess
gafas	glasses
hospital	hospital
infectado	septic
inyección	injection
medicina	medicine
médico	doctor
oculista	optician
otorrinolaringólogo	ear, nose and throat specialist
radiografía	X-ray
receta	prescription
reconocimiento	check-up
tensión	blood pressure
Urgencias	Emergencies

CONVERSION TABLES

DISTANCES

Distances are marked in kilometres. To convert kilometres to miles, divide the km. by 8 and multiply by 5 (one km. being five-eighths of a mile). Convert miles to km. by dividing the miles by 5 and multiplying by 8. A mile is 1609m. (1.609km.).

km.	miles or km.	miles
1.61	1	0.62
3.22	2	1.24
4.83	3	1.86
6.44	4	2.48
8.05	5	3.11
9.66	6	3.73
11.27	7	4.35
12.88	8	4.97
14.49	9	5.59
16.10	10	6.21
32.20	20	12.43
48.28	30	18.64
64.37	40	24.85
80.47	50	31.07
160.93	100	62.14
321.90	200	124.30
804.70	500	310.70
1609.34	1000	621.37

Other units of length:

1 centimetre	= 0.39 in.	1 inch	= 25.4 millimetres
1 metre	= 39.37 in.	1 foot	= 0.30 metre (30 cm.)
10 metres	= 32.81 ft.	1 yard	= 0.91 metre

CONVERSION TABLES

WEIGHTS

The unit you will come into most contact with is the kilogram (kilo), equivalent to 2 lb 3 oz. To convert kg. to lbs., multiply by 2 and add one-tenth of the result (thus, 6 kg x 2 = 12 + 1.2, or 13.2 lbs). One ounce is about 28 grams, and 1 lb is 454 g. One UK hundredweight is almost 51 kg; one USA cwt is 45 kg. One UK ton is 1016 kg (USA ton = 907 kg).

grams	ounces	ounces	grams
50	1.76	1	28.3
100	3.53	2	56.7
250	8.81	4	113.4
500	17.63	8	226.8

kg.	lbs. or kg.	lbs.
0.45	1	2.20
0.91	2	4.41
1.36	3	6.61
1.81	4	8.82
2.27	5	11.02
2.72	6	13.23
3.17	7	15.43
3.63	8	17.64
4.08	9	19.84
4.53	10	22.04
9.07	20	44.09
11.34	25	55.11
22.68	50	110.23
45.36	100	220.46

LIQUIDS

Motorists from the UK will be used to seeing petrol priced per litre (and may even know that one litre is about $1\frac{3}{4}$ pints). One 'imperial' gallon is roughly $4\frac{1}{2}$ litres, but USA drivers must remember that the American gallon is only 3.8 litres (1 litre = 1.06 US quart). In the following table, imperial gallons are used:

litres	gals. or l.	gals.
4.54	1	0.22
9.10	2	0.44
13.64	3	0.66
18.18	4	0.88
22.73	5	1.10
27.27	6	1.32
31.82	7	1.54
36.37	8	1.76
40.91	9	1.98
45.46	10	2.20
90.92	20	4.40
136.38	30	6.60
181.84	40	8.80
227.30	50	11.00

TYRE PRESSURES

lb/sq.in.	15	18	20	22	24
kg/sq.cm.	1.1	1.3	1.4	1.5	1.7

lb/sq.in.	26	28	30	33	35
kg/sq.cm.	1.8	2.0	2.1	2.3	2.5

AREA

The average tourist isn't all that likely to need metric area conversions, but with more 'holiday home' plots being bought overseas nowadays it might be useful to know that 1 square metre = 10.8 square feet, and that the main unit of land area measurement is a hectare (which is $2\frac{1}{2}$ acres). The hectare is 10,000 sq.m. – for convenience, visualise something roughly 100 metres or yards square. To convert hectares to acres, divide by 2 and multiply by 5 (and vice-versa).

hectares	acres or ha.	acres
0.4	**1**	2.5
2.0	**5**	12.4
4.1	**10**	24.7
20.2	**50**	123.6
40.5	**100**	247.1

TEMPERATURE

To convert centigrade or Celsius degrees into Fahrenheit, the accurate method is to multiply the °C figure by 1.8 and add 32. Similarly, to convert °F to °C, subtract 32 from the °F figure and divide by 1.8. This will give you a truly accurate conversion, but takes a little time in mental arithmetic! See the table below. If all you want is some idea of how hot it is forecast to be in the sun, simply double the °C figure and add 30; the °F result will be overstated by a degree or two when the answer is in the 60-80°F range, while 90°F should be 86°F.

°C	°F	°C	°F	
-10	14	25	77	
0	32	30	86	
5	41	36.9	98.4	body temperature
10	50	40	104	
20	68	100	212	boiling point

CLOTHING SIZES

Slight variations in sizes, let alone European equivalents of UK/USA
sizes, will be found everywhere so be sure to check before you buy.
The following tables are approximate:

Women's dresses and suits

UK	10	12	14	16	18	20
Europe	**36**	**38**	**40**	**42**	**44**	**46**
USA	8	10	12	14	16	18

Men's suits and coats

UK/USA	36	38	40	42	44	46
Europe	**46**	**48**	**50**	**52**	**54**	**56**

Women's shoes

UK	4	5	6	7	8
Europe	**37**	**38**	**39**	**41**	**42**
USA	$5\frac{1}{2}$	$6\frac{1}{2}$	$7\frac{1}{2}$	$8\frac{1}{2}$	$9\frac{1}{2}$

Men's shoes

UK/USA	7	8	9	10	11
Europe	**41**	**42**	**43**	**44**	**45**

Men's shirts

UK/USA	14	$14\frac{1}{2}$	15	$15\frac{1}{2}$	16	$16\frac{1}{2}$	17
Europe	**36**	**37**	**38**	**39**	**41**	**42**	**43**

Women's sweaters

UK/USA	32	34	36	38	40
Europe	**36**	**38**	**40**	**42**	**44**

Waist and chest measurements

Inches	28	30	32	34	36	38	40	42	44	46
Cms	71	76	80	87	91	97	102	107	112	117

MINI—DICTIONARY

accelerator el acelerador
accident un accidente
accommodation el alojamiento
ache un dolor
adaptor *(electrical)* el adaptador
address la dirección
adhesive el pegamento
after después de
after-shave el after-shave
again otra vez
against contra
air el aire
air-conditioning el aire
  acondicionado
aircraft el avión
air freshener el ambientador
air hostess la azafata
airline la compañía aérea
airport el aeropuerto
alcohol el alcohol
all todo
almost casi
alone solo
already ya
always siempre
am: I am soy
ambulance la ambulancia
America América
American americano
and y
ankle el tobillo
anorak el anorak
another otro
anti-freeze el anticongelante
antique shop la tienda de
  antigüedades
antiseptic un antiséptico
aperitif el aperitivo
appendicitis una apendicitis

appetite el apetito
apple la manzana
application form un impreso de
  solicitud
appointment *(with hairdresser)*
  hora   *(business etc)* una cita
apricot el albaricoque
are: are you Spanish? ¿es usted
  español?
  we are English somos ingleses
  they are mine son mios
arm el brazo
art el arte
art gallery el museo de Bellas
  Artes
artist el artista
ashtray el cenicero
asleep dormido
aspirin una aspirina
at: at night por la noche
  at 3 o'clock a las tres
  at the post office en Correos
attractive *(woman)* guapa
  (offer etc) atractivo
aunt una tía
Australia Australia
Australian australiano
Austria Austria
Austrian austríaco
automatic automático
away: is it far away? ¿está lejos?
  go away! ¡lárguese!
awful horrible
axe el hacha
axle el eje

baby el niño pequeño

back *(at the back)* detrás
  (body) la espalda
  come back! ¡vuelva!
bacon el bacon
  bacon and eggs huevos fritos
  con bacon
bad malo
bait el cebo
bake cocer al horno
baker el panadería
balcony el balcón
ball *(for playing)* la pelota
  (dance) el baile
ball-point pen el bolígrafo
banana el plátano
band *(of cloth etc)* una tira
  (musicians) una banda
bandage la venda
bank el banco
banknote el billete de banco
bar el bar
  bar of chocolate una tableta
  de chocolate
barbecue la barbacoa
barber's la peluquería de
  caballeros
bargain una ganga
basement el sótano
basin el lavabo
basket el cesto
bath el baño
bathing hat el gorro de baño
bathroom el cuarto de baño
bath salts las sales de baño
battery *(car)* la batería
  (torch etc) la pila
beach la playa
beach ball el balón de playa
beans las judías
  (broad) las habas
beard la barba
because porque

bed la cama
bed linen la ropa de cama
bedroom el dormitorio
beef la carne de vaca
beer la cerveza
before antes
beginner un principiante
behind detrás
beige beige
bell *(church)* la campana
  (door) el timbre
belt el cinturón
beside al lado de
better mejor
between entre
bicycle la bicicleta
big grande
bikini el bikini
bill la cuenta
  (invoice) la factura
bin liner la bolsa de basura
bird el pájaro
birthday el cumpleaños
  happy birthday! ¡felicidades!
birthday card la tarjeta de
  felicitación
biscuit una galleta
bite *(insect)* una picadura
  (dog) una mordedura
bitter amargo
black negro
blackberries *(fruit)* las moras
  blackberry jam mermelada de
  moras
blackcurrants las grosellas
  negras
  blackcurrant juice zumo de
  grosella
blanket la manta
bleach *(verb)* blanquear
  (noun) la lejía
blind *(cannot see)* ciego

(window) la persiana
blister una ampolla
blood la sangre
blouse la blusa
blue azul
boat el barco
  (smaller) la barca
body el cuerpo
  (corpse) el cadáver
boil *(verb)* hervir
  (noun) el forúnculo
bolt *(verb)* echar el cerrojo
  (noun: on door) el cerrojo
bone el hueso
  (fish) una espina
bonnet *(car)* el capó
book *(noun)* el libro
  (verb) reservar
  I'll book the tickets yo sacaré
  los billetes
booking office *(railway station)*
  el despacho de billetes
  (theatre etc) la taquilla
bookshop la librería
boot *(car)* el maletero
  (footwear) la bota
border el borde
  (between countries) la frontera
boring aburrido
born: I was born in... nací
  en...
both: both of them los dos
  both... and... tanto... como
bottle la botella
bottle-opener el abrebotellas
bottom el fondo
bowl el cuenco
box la caja
boy el chico
boyfriend el novio
bra el sostén
bracelet la pulsera

braces los tirantes
brake *(noun)* el freno
  (verb) frenar
brandy el coñac
bread el pan
breakdown *(car)* una avería
  (nervous) una crisis nerviosa
breakfast el desayuno
breathe respirar
  I can't breathe no puedo
  respirar
bridge el puente
briefcase la cartera
brochure el folleto
broken roto
brooch el broche
brother el hermano
brown *(hair, tanned)* moreno
  (colour) marrón
bruise un cardenal
brush *(noun)* el cepillo
  (verb) cepillar
bucket el cubo
building el edificio
bumper el parachoques
burn *(verb)* quemar
  (noun) una quemadura
bus el autobús
business el negocio
  it's none of your business no
  es asunto suyo
busker un músico callejero
bus station la estación de
  autobuses
busy ocupado
but pero
butcher la carnicería
butter la mantequilla
button el botón
buy comprar
by: by the door junto a la puerta
  by Friday para el viernes

by myself yo solo

cabbage la col
cable car el teleférico
cafe el café
cagoule el chubasquero
cake *(small)* el pastel
  (large) la tarta
  sponge cake el bizcocho
cake shop la pastelería
calculator la calculadora
camera la máquina de fotos
campsite el camping
camshaft el árbol de levas
can *(able)* poder
  (tin) una lata
  can I have a...? ¿me da un...?
canal el canal
candle la vela
canoe la piragua
cap la gorra
car el coche
caravan la caravana
carburettor el carburador
card la tarjeta
cardigan la rebeca
careful prudente
  be careful! ¡cuidado!
carpet la alfombra
carriage *(train)* el vagón
carrot la zanahoria
carry-cot el capazo
case la maleta
cash el dinero
  (verb: a cheque) cobrar
  to pay cash pagar al contado
cassette la cassette
cassette player el cassette
castle el castillo
cat el gato

cathedral la catedral
cauliflower la coliflor
cave la cueva
cemetery el cementerio
certificate el certificado
chair la silla
chambermaid la camarera
chamber music la música de
  Cámara
change *(verb)* *(money)* cambiar
  (of clothes) cambiarse
cheap barato
cheers! ¡salud!
cheese el queso
chemist *(shop)* la farmacia
cheque el cheque
cheque book el talonario de
  cheques
cheque card la tarjeta de banco
cherries las cerezas
  cherry jam mermelada de
  cereza
chess el adjedrez
chest el pecho
chewing gum el chicle
chicken *(cooked)* el pollo
child el niño/la niña
  children los niños
chips las patatas fritas
chocolate el chocolate
  box of chocolates una caja de
  bombones
chop *(food)* la chuleta
  (to cut) cortar
church la iglesia
cigar el (cigarro) puro
cigarette el cigarrillo
cinema el cine
city la ciudad
city centre el centro (urbano)
class la clase
classical music la música clásica

clean limpio
clear claro
  is that clear? ¿está claro?
clever listo
  it was very clever of you lo
  hizo usted muy bien
clock el reloj
close *(near)* cerca
  (stuffy) sofocante
close *(verb)* cerrar
  the shop is closed la tienda
  está cerrada
clothes la ropa
club *(society)* el club
  (golf etc) el palo
  (cards) tréboles
clutch el embrague
coach el autobús
  (of train) el vagón
coach station la estación de
  autobuses
coat el abrigo
coathanger la percha
cockroach la cucaracha
coffee el café
coin la moneda
cold *(illness)* un resfriado
  (adj) frío
collar el cuello
  (of animal) el collar
collection *(stamps etc)* la
  colección
  (postal) la recogida
colour el color
colour film un carrete en color
comb *(noun)* el peine
  (verb) peinar
come venir
  I come from... soy de...
  we came last week llegamos
  la semana pasada
communication cord la alarma

compact disc el disco compacto
compartment el compartimento
complicated complicado
concert el concierto
conditioner *(hair)* la crema
  acondicionadora
conductor *(bus)* el cobrador
  (orchestra) el director
congratulations! ¡enhorabuena!
constipation estreñimiento
consulate el consulado
contact lenses las lentes de
  contacto
contraceptive un anticonceptivo
cook *(noun)* el cocinero
  (verb) guisar
cooking utensils los utensilios
  de cocina
cool *(adj)* fresco
  (verb) refrescar
corkscrew el sacacorchos
corner *(of street)* la esquina
  (of room) el rincón
corridor el pasillo
cosmetics los cosméticos
cost *(verb)* costar
  what does it cost? ¿cuánto
  cuesta?
cotton el algodón
cotton wool el algodón
cough *(noun)* la tos
  (verb) toser
council el consejo
  (city) el ayuntamiento
country *(state)* el país
  (not town) el campo
cousin *(male)* el primo
  (female) la prima
crab el cangrejo
cramp un calambre
crayfish las cigalas
cream *(for cake etc)* la nata

(pudding, lotion) la crema
credit card la tarjeta de crédito
crew la tripulación
crisps las patatas fritas (a la inglesa)
crowded lleno
  it was very crowded había muchísima gente
cruise el crucero
crutches las muletas
cry llorar
  (shout) gritar
cucumber el pepino
cufflinks los gemelos
cup la taza
cupboard el armario
curlers los rulos
curry el curry
curtain la cortina
cut *(noun)* una cortadura
  (verb) cortar

dad papá
dairy *(shop)* la lechería
dark oscuro
daughter la hija
day el día
dead muerto
deaf sordo
dear *(expensive)* caro
  (cherished) querido
deckchair la tumbona
deep profundo
deliberately a propósito
dentist el dentista
dentures la dentadura postiza
deny: I deny it lo niego
deodorant el desodorante
department store los grandes almacenes

departure la salida
develop *(grow)* desarrollarse
  (a film) revelar
diamonds *(jewels)* los diamantes
  (cards) carreau
diarrhoea una diarrea
diary el diario
  (engagement) la agenda
dictionary el diccionario
die morir
diesel el diesel
  (oil) el gas-oil
different: that's different eso es distinto
  I'd like a different one quería otro distinto
difficult difícil
dining car el vagón-comedor
dining room el comedor
directory la guía
  (telephone) la guía telefónica
dirty sucio
disabled minusválido
distributor *(car)* el distribuidor
dive *(into water)* zambullirse
  (under water) bucear
diving board el trampolín
divorced divorciado
do hacer
doctor el médico
document el documento
dog el perro
doll la muñeca
dollar el dólar
door la puerta
double room una habitación doble
doughnut un rosco
down hacia abajo
  (position) abajo
  to go down bajar
drawing pin una chincheta

dress el vestido
drink *(verb)* beber
  (noun) una bebida
  would you like a drink?
  ¿quiere beber algo?
drinking water agua potable
drive *(verb: car)* conducir
driver el conductor
driving licence el carnet de
  conducir
drunk borracho
dry seco
dry-cleaner la tintorería
during durante
dustbin el cubo de la basura
duster el trapo del polvo
duty-free shop la tienda libre de
  impuestos

each *(every)* cada
  two pounds each dos libras
  cada uno
early temprano
earrings los pendientes
ears *(outside)* las orejas
  (inside) los oídos
east el Este
easy fácil
egg el huevo
egg cup la huevera
either: either of them
  cualquiera de ellos
  either... or... o bien... o...
elastic elástico
elastic band una gomita
elbows los codos
electric eléctrico
electricity la electricidad
else: something else algo más
  someone else alguien más

  somewhere else en otro sitio
embarrassing violento
  it was most embarrassing
  me daba mucha vergüenza
embassy la embajada
embroidery el bordado
emerald la esmeralda
emergency una emergencia
empty vacío
end el final
engaged *(couple)* prometidos
  (occupied) ocupado
engine *(motor)* el motor
  (railway) la locomotora
England Inglaterra
English inglés
enlargement una ampliación
enough bastante
  that's enough ¡basta ya!
entertainment las diversiones
entrance la entrada
envelope el sobre
escalator la escalera mecánica
especially sobre todo
Europe Europa
European europeo
evening la tarde
  (after dark) la noche
every cada
  every year todos los años
everyone todos
everything todo
everywhere por todas partes
example un ejemplo
  for example por ejemplo
excellent excelente
excess baggage exceso de
  equipaje
exchange *(verb)* cambiar
exchange rate el cambio
excursion la excursión
excuse me! ¡perdón!

(getting past) ¡por favor!
exit *(noun)* la salida
expensive caro
extension lead el cable
  alargador
eye drops un colirio
eyes los ojos

face la cara
faint *(unclear)* tenue
  (verb) desmayarse
  to feel faint sentirse débil
fair *(funfair)* la feria
  (just) justo
  it's not fair no hay derecho
false teeth la dentadura postiza
fan *(ventilator)* el ventilador
  (enthusiast) un fan
  (hand fan) el abanico
fan belt la correa del ventilador
far lejos
fare el billete
farm la granja
farmer el granjero
fashion la moda
fast rápido
  (colour) resistente
fat *(of person)* gordo
  (on meat etc) la grasa
father el padre
feel *(touch)* tocar
  I feel tired me encuentro
    cansado
  I feel like... me apetece...
  I don't feel well no me
    encuentro bien
feet los pies
felt-tip pen un rotulador
ferry el ferry
fever fiebre

fiancé el prometido
fiancée la prometida
field el campo
figs los higos
filling *(tooth)* el empaste
  (sandwich etc) el relleno
film la película
finger el dedo
fire el fuego
  (accidental) el incendio
fire extinguisher el extintor
fireworks los fuegos artificiales
first primero
  first-aid primeros auxilios
first floor el primer piso
fish el pez
  (food) el pescado
fishing la pesca
  to to fishing ir a pescar
fishing rod la caña de pescar
fishmonger la pescadería
fizzy con burbujas
flag la bandera
flash *(camera)* el flash
flat *(level)* plano
  (apartment) el piso
flavour el sabor
flight el vuelo
flip-flops las sandalias de goma
flippers las aletas
flour la harina
flower la flor
flu la gripe
flute la flauta
fly *(verb)* volar
  (insect) la mosca
fog la niebla
folk music la música folklórica
food la comida
food poisoning una intoxicación
  alimenticia
foot el pie

football *(game)* el fútbol
  (ball) el balón
for: for me para mí
  what for? ¿para qué?
  for a week una semana
foreigner un extranjero
forest el bosque
  (tropical) la selva
fork el tenedor
fortnight una quincena
fountain pen la (pluma) estilográfica
fracture una fractura
France Francia
free *(no cost)* gratis
  (at liberty) libre
freezer el congelador
French francés
fridge el frigorífico
friend el amigo
friendly simpático
front: in front delante
frost la escarcha
fruit la fruta
fruit juice un zumo de frutas
fry freír
frying pan la sartén
full lleno
full board pensión completa
funnel *(for pouring)* el embudo
funny divertido
  (strange) raro
furniture los muebles

garage *(to park car)* el garage
  (for repairs) el taller
garden el jardín
garlic el ajo
gas-permeable lenses las lentes de contacto semi-rígidas

gay *(happy)* alegre
  (homosexual) gay
gear el equipo
  (car) la marcha
gear lever la palanca de velocidades
gents *(toilet)* los servicios de caballeros
German alemán
Germany Alemania
get *(fetch)* traer
  have you got?... ¿tiene...?
  to get the train coger el tren
get back
  to get sth. back recobrar algo
  we get back tomorrow nos volvemos mañana
get in *(car)* subirse a
  (arrive) llegar
get out bajarse de
  (bring out) sacar
get up *(rise)* levantarse
gift el regalo
gin la ginebra
ginger el jengibre
girl la chica
girlfriend la novia
give dar
glad alegre
glass el vaso
  (material) cristal
  I'm glad me alegro
glasses las gafas
gloss prints las copias en brillo
gloves los guantes
glue el pegamento
goggles las gafas de bucear
gold el oro
good bueno
goodbye adiós
government el gobierno
grapes las uvas

grass la hierba
green verde
grey gris
grill la parrilla
grocer *(shop)* la tienda de comestibles
ground floor la planta baja
ground sheet la lona impermeable
guarantee *(noun)* la garantía
(verb) garantizar
guard el guarda
guide book la guía turística
guitar la guitarra
gun *(rifle)* la escopeta
(pistol) la pistola

hair el pelo
hair dryer el secador (de pelo)
hair spray la laca
haircut el corte de pelo
hairdresser el peluquero
  to go to the hairdresser ir a la peluquería
half medio
  half an hour media hora
half board media pensión
ham el jamón
hamburger la hamburguesa
hammer el martillo
hand la mano
handbag el bolso
hand brake el freno de mano
handkerchief el pañuelo
handle *(door)* el picaporte
handsome guapo
(profit etc) considerble
hangover la resaca
happy feliz
(contented) contento

harbour el puerto
hard duro
(difficult) difícil
hard lenses las lentes de contacto duras
hat el sombrero
(wool) el gorro
have *(own)* tener
  I have to go tengo que irme
  can I have...? ¿me da...?
  do you have...? ¿tiene...?
hayfever la fiebre del heno
he él
head la cabeza
headache un dolor de cabeza
headlights los faros
hear oír
  I can't hear no oigo
hearing aid el audífono
heart el corazón
(cards) corazones
  heart attack un infarto
heating la calefacción
heavy pesado
  it's very heavy pesa mucho
heel el talón
(shoes) el tacón
hello hola
(to get attention) ¡oiga!
help *(noun)* la ayuda
(verb) ayudar
  help! ¡socorro!
her: it's her es ella
  it's for her es para ella
  give it to her déselo
her su
  it's hers es suyo
here aquí
hi ¡hola!
high alto
highway code el código de carretera

hill el monte
  uphill cuesta arriba
him: it's him es él
  it's for him es para él
  give it to him déselo
his su
  it's his es suyo
history la historia
hitch-hike hacer auto-stop
hobby el hobby
holiday las vacaciones
honest honrado
  (sincere) sincero
honey la miel
honeymoon el viaje de novios
horn *(car)* el claxon
  (animal) el cuerno
horrible horrible
hospital el hospital
hot caliente
  it's hot hace calor
hot water bottle la bolsa de
  agua caliente
hour la hora
house la casa
how? ¿cómo?
hungry: I'm hungry tengo
  hambre
husband el marido

I yo
ice el hielo
ice cream el helado
ice cube un cubito de hielo
ice lolly el polo
if si
ignition el encendido
immediately inmediatamente
impossible imposible
in en

indicator el indicador
indigestion una indigestión
infection una infección
information la información
injection la inyección
injury la herida
ink la tinta
inn la fonda
inner tube la cámara (neumática)
insect el insecto
insect repellent la loción anti-
  mosquitos
insomnia el insomnio
insurance el seguro
interesting interesante
invitation la invitación
Ireland Irlanda
Irish irlandés
iron *(metal)* el hierro
  (for clothes) la plancha
ironmonger la ferretería
is: he/she/it is es
island la isla
Italian italiano
Italy Italia
itch *(noun)* un picor
  (verb) picar
  it itches me pica

jacket la chaqueta
jacuzzi el baño de masaje
jam la mermelada
jazz el jazz
jealous *(in love)* celoso
  she makes me jealous me da
  envidia
jeans los tejanos
jellyfish una medusa
jeweller la joyería
job el trabajo

jog *(verb)* hacer footing
  to go for a jog ir de footing
joke una broma
  (story) el chiste
  you're joking ¿lo dice en serio?
journey el viaje
jumper el jersey
just: it's just arrived acaba de llegar
  I've just one left sólo me queda uno

key la llave
kidney el riñón
kilo un kilo
kilometre un kilómetro
kitchen la cocina
knees las rodillas
knife el cuchillo
knit hacer punto
knitting needle la aguja de punto

label la etiqueta
lace el encaje
  (of shoe) el cordón
ladies *(toilet)* los servicios de señoras
lake el lago
lamb el cordero
lamp la lámpara
lampshade la pantalla
land *(noun)* la tierra
  (verb) aterrizar
language el idioma
large grande
last *(final)* último

last month/year el mes/el año pasado
  at last! ¡por fin!
late: it's getting late se está haciendo tarde
  the bus is late el autobús se ha retrasado
laugh reír
launderette la lavandería automática
laundry *(dirty)* la ropa sucia
  (washed) la colada
laxative un laxante
lazy perezoso
leaf la hoja
learn aprender
leather el cuero
left *(not right)* izquierdo
  (remaining) restante
  there's nothing left no queda nada
left luggage la consigna
leg la pierna
lemon el limón
lemonade la limonada
length la longitud
lens la lente
lesson la clase
letter *(post)* la carta
  (alphabet) la letra
letterbox el buzón
lettuce la lechuga
library la biblioteca
licence el permiso
life la vida
lift el ascensor
  to give s.o. a lift llevar a alguien en coche
light *(not heavy)* ligero
  (not dark) claro
lighter el encendedor
lighter fuel el gas para el

encendedor
light meter el contador de la luz
like: I like it me gusta
  what's it like? ¿cómo es?
lime *(fruit)* la lima
lip salve la crema labial
lipstick la barra de labios
liqueur el licor
list la lista
litre un litro
litter la basura
little *(small)* pequeño
  it's a little big es un poco
  grande
liver el hígado
lobster la langosta
lollipop el chupa-chup
lorry el camión
lost property los objetos
  perdidos
lot: a lot mucho
loud alto
  (colour) chillón
lounge *(in house)* el cuarto de
  estar
  (in hotel etc) el salón
low bajo
  (voice) baja
luck la suerte
  good luck! ¡suerte!
luggage el equipaje
luggage rack la rejilla de
  equipajes
lunch la comida

magazine la revista
mail el correo
make hacer
man el hombre
manager el gerente

(hotel) el director
map el mapa
margarine la margarina
market el mercado
marmalade la mermelada de
  naranja
married casado(s)
mascara el rímel
mass *(church)* la misa
match *(light)* la cerilla
  (sport) el partido
material *(cloth)* la tela
mattress el colchón
maybe quizás
me: it's me soy yo
  it's for me es para mí
  give it to me démelo
meal la comida
meat la carne
mechanic el mecánico
medicine la medicina
meeting la reunión
melon el melón
menu la carta
message el recado
midday mediodía
middle *(in the middle)* en el
  centro
  the middle house la casa de
  en medio
midnight medianoche
milk la leche
mine mío
  it's mine es mío
mineral water el agua mineral
mirror el espejo
mistake la equivocación
  to make a mistake
  equivocarse
money el dinero
month el mes
monument el monumento

moped el ciclomotor
morning la mañana
  in the morning por la mañana
mother la madre
motorbike la motocicleta
motorboat la motora
motorway la autopista
mountain la montaña
moustache el bigote
mouth la boca
move mover
  don't move no se mueva
much: not much no mucho
mug la jarrita
mum mamá
museum el museo
mushrooms *(as food)* los champiñones
music la música
musical instrument el instrumento musical
musician el músico
mussels los mejillones
mustard la mostaza
my mi
  that's my book ese libro es mío

nail *(metal)* la lima
  (finger) la uña
nail file la lima de uñas
nail polish el esmalte de uñas
narrow estrecho
near cerca
  near the door junto a la puerta
neck el cuello
necklace el collar
need *(verb)* necesitar
need: I need... necesito...

there's no need no hace falta
needle la aguja
negative *(photo)* el negativo
  (answer) una negativa
neither: neither of them ninguno de ellos
  neither... nor... ni... ni...
nephew el sobrino
never nunca
new *(not old)* nuevo
news las noticias
newsagent el kiosko de periódicos
New Zealand Nueva Zelanda
New Zealander neozelandés
next *(following)* siguiente
  next week/month la semana/el mes que viene
  what next? ¿y ahora qué?
niece la sobrina
night la noche
nightclub el night club
nightdress el camisón
no *(response)* no
  (not any) ningún
noisy ruidoso
north el norte
  north of the town al norte de la ciudad
nose la nariz
nose drops las gotas nasales
not no
notebook el cuaderno
novel la novela
now ahora
nudist nudista
number el número
number plate la matrícula
nurse la enfermera
nut *(fruit)* la nuez
  (& bolt) la tuerca

occasionally de vez en cuando
office la oficina
often a menudo
oil el aceite
ointment la pomada
old viejo
  how old is he? ¿cuántos años
  tiene?
olive *(fruit)* la aceituna
  (tree) el olivo
  olive oil el aceite de oliva
omelette la tortilla
on en
onion la cebolla
open *(verb)* abrir
  (adj) abierto
operator *(phone)* la operadora
opposite enfrente de
optician el oculista
or o
orange *(colour)* naranja
  (fruit) la naranja
orchestra la orquesta
organ el órgano
our nuestro
  it's ours es nuestro
out: he's out no está
outside fuera
  outside the room fuera de la
  habitación
over encima de
  over here por aquí
overtake adelantar
oysters las ostras

package el paquete
  a packet of... una cajetilla
  de...
packet el paquete
pack of cards la baraja

page la página
pain el dolor
pair el par
pancake una crepe
paracetamol el paracetamol
paraffin la parafina
parasol la sombrilla
parcel el paquete
parents los padres
pardon? ¿como dice?
park *(noun)* el parque
  (verb) aparcar
parsley el perejil
party *(celebration)* la fiesta
  (group) el grupo
passenger el pasajero
passport el pasaporte
pasta las pastas
path el camino
pay pagar
peach el melocotón
peanuts los cacahuetes
pear la pera
pearl la perla
peas los guisantes
pedestrian el peatón
  pedestrian crossing el paso
  de peatones
peg *(clothes)* la pinza
pen la pluma
  I don't have a pen no tengo
  bolígrafo
pencil el lápiz
pencil sharpener el sacapuntas
penfriend un amigo por
  correspondencia
penknife la navaja
pepper *(& salt)* la pimienta
  (red/green) el pimiento
peppermints las pastillas de
  menta
perfume el perfume

perhaps quizás
perm una permanente
petrol la gasolina
petrol station la gasolinera
petticoat la combinación
photograph *(noun)* la foto(grafía)
  (verb) fotografiar
photographer el fotógrafo
phrase book el libro de frases
piano el piano
pickpocket un carterista
picnic el picnic
  to go for a picnic ir a comer
  al campo
piece un pedazo
pillow la almohada
pilot el piloto
pin el alfiler
pineapple la piña
pink rosa
pipe *(for smoking)* la pipa
  (for water) la tubería
piston el pistón
piston ring un segmento de
  pistón
pizza la pizza
plant la planta
plaster la escayola
plastic el plástico
  plastic bag una bolsa de
  plástico
plate el plato
platform el andén
please por favor
plug *(electrical)* el enchufe
  (sink) el tapón
pocket el bolsillo
poison el veneno
policeman el policía
police station la comisaría
politics la política
poor pobre

(bad quality) malo
pop music la música moderna
pork la carne de cerdo
port *(harbour)* el puerto
  (drink) un Oporto
porter *(hotel)* el conserje
  (station) el mozo
Portugal Portugal
Portuguese portugués
post *(noun)* el correo
  (verb) echar al buzón
post box el buzón
postcard la postal
poster el poster
postman el cartero
post office (la oficina de)
  Correos
potato la patata
poultry las aves
pound *(money, weight)* la libra
powder el polvo
  (cosmetics) los polvos
pram el cochecito
prawns las gambas
prescription la receta
pretty *(beautiful)* bonito
  (quite) bastante
priest el cura
private privado
problem el problema
  what's the problem? ¿qué
  pasa?
public público
pull tirar de
  pull ¡tire!
purple morado
purse el monedero
push empujar
pushchair la sillita de ruedas
pyjamas el pijama

quality la calidad
quay el muelle
question *(noun)* la pregunta
  (verb: police) interrogar
  the question of... la cuestión
  de...
queue *(noun)* la cola
  (verb) hacer cola
quick rápido
quiet tranquilo
  (person) callado
quilt el edredón
quite bastante

radiator el radiador
radio la radio
radish el rábano
  (small red) la rabanilla
railway line la vía (férrea)
rain la lluvia
raincoat la gabardina
raisins las pasas
rare *(uncommon)* raro
  (steak) poco pasado
raspberries las frambuesas
  raspberry ice cream helado
  de frambuesa
razor blades las cuchillas de
  afeitar
reading lamp la lámpara para
  leer
ready listo
rear lights las luces traseras
receipt el recibo
receptionist el/la recepcionista
record *(musical)* el disco
  (sporting etc) el record
record player el tocadiscos
record shop la tienda de discos
red rojo

refreshments los refrescos
registered letter una carta
  certificada
relax relajarse
  (rest) descansar
religion la religión
remember recordar
  I don't remember him no
  me acuerdo de él
reservation la reserva
rest *(remainder)* el resto
  (relax) descansar
restaurant el restaurante
restaurant car el
  vagón-restaurante
return *(come back)* volver
  (give back) devolver
rice el arroz
rich rico
right *(correct)* correcto
  (direction) derecha
ring *(to call)* llamar por teléfono
  (wedding etc) el anillo
ripe maduro
river el río
road la carretera
rock *(stone)* una roca
  (music) el Rock
roll *(bread)* un bollo
  (verb) rodar
roller skates los patines
room *(in building)* la habitación
  (space) sitio
rope la cuerda
rose la rosa
round *(circular)* redondo
  it's my round me toca a mí
rowing boat la barca de remos
rubber *(eraser)* la goma (de
  borrar)
  (material) la goma
rubbish la basura

rubbish! ¡tonterías!
ruby *(colour)* rojo rubí
rucksack la mochila
rug *(mat)* la alfombra
  (blanket) la manta
ruins las ruinas
ruler la regla
rum el ron
runway la pista

sad triste
safe seguro
  is it safe? ¿no hay peligro?
safety pin el imperdible
sailing boat el balandro
salad la ensalada
sale la venta
  (at reduced prices) las rebajas
salmon el salmón
salt la sal
same el mismo
  it's the same da lo mismo
sand la arena
sand dunes las dunas
sandals las sandalias
sandwich un bocadillo
  (toasted) un sandwich
sanitary towels las compresas
sauce la salsa
saucepan el cazo
sauna la sauna
sausage la salchicha
say: what did you say? ¿qué ha dicho?
  how do you say...? ¿cómo se dice...?
scampi las gambas
Scandinavia Escandinavia
scarf la bufanda
  (head) el pañuelo

school la escuela
scissors las tijeras
Scotland Escocia
Scottish escocés
screw el tornillo
screwdriver el destornillador
sea el mar
seat el asiento
seat belt el cinturón de seguridad
see ver
  I can't see no veo
  I see ya
sell vender
sellotape ® el papel Cello ®
serious serio
serviette la servilleta
several varios
sew coser
shampoo el champú
  (at the hairdresser) un lavado
shave *(verb)* afeitar(se)
  (noun) un afeitado
shaving foam la espuma de afeitar
shawl el chal
she ella
sheet la sábana
  (of paper etc) la hoja
shell la concha
  (of egg etc) la cáscara
  shellfish mariscos
sherry el jerez
ship el barco
shirt la camisa
shoe laces los cordones de los zapatos
shoe polish la crema de zapatos
shoes los zapatos
shoe shop la zapatería
shop la tienda
shopping *(noun)* la compra

to go shopping ir de compras
shopping centre el centro comercial
short corto
shorts los pantalones cortos
shoulder el hombro
shower *(bath)* la ducha
  (rain) el chaparrón
shrimps las quisquillas
shutter *(camera)* el obturador
  (window) el postigo
sick *(ill)* enfermo
  to feel sick sentir náuseas
side *(edge)* el borde
  (page) el lado
  I'm on his side estoy de parte suya
sidelights las luces de posición
silk la seda
silver *(colour)* plateado
  (metal) la plata
simple sencillo
sing cantar
single *(one)* único
  (unmarried) soltero
single room una habitación individual
sister la hermana
skid *(verb)* patinar
skin cleanser la leche limpiadora
skirt la falda
sky el cielo
sleep *(noun)* el sueño
  (verb) dormir
  to go to sleep dormirse
sleeping bag el saco de dormir
sleeping car el coche-cama
sleeping pill un somnífero
sling *(noun: med)* el cabestrillo
slippers las zapatillas
slow lento

to go slow ir despacio
small pequeño
smell *(noun)* el olor
smile *(noun)* la sonrisa
  (verb) sonreír
smoke *(noun)* el humo
  (verb) fumar
snack un bocadillo
  we went for a snack fuimos a tomar algo
snorkel el respirador
snow la nieve
so tan
  (therefore) entonces
soaking solution *(for contact lenses)* la solución limpiadora
soap el jabón
socks los calcetines
soda water el agua de seltz
soft lenses las lentes de contacto blandas
somebody alguien
somehow de algún modo
something algo
sometimes a veces
somewhere en alguna parte
son el hijo
song la canción
sorry: I'm sorry perdón
soup la sopa
south el sur
  south of the town al sur de la ciudad
South America Sudamérica
souvenir un recuerdo
spade *(shovel)* la pala
  (cards) picas
Spain España
Spanish español
spanner la llave inglesa
spares los repuestos
spark(ing) plug la bujía

speak hablar
  do you speak...? ¿habla...?
  I don't speak... no hablo...
speed la velocidad
speed limit el límite de
  velocidad
speedometer el cuentakilómetros
spider la araña
spinach las espinacas
spoon la cuchara
sprain *(noun)* una torcedura
spring *(mechanical)* el muelle
  (season) la primavera
stadium el estadio
staircase la escalera
stairs las escaleras
stamp el sello
stapler la grapadora
star la estrella
start *(noun)* el principio
  (verb) empezar
station la estación
statue la estatua
steak el filete
steamer el vapor
steering wheel el volante
steward *(in aircraft)* el aeromozo
sting *(noun)* una picadura
  (verb) picar
  it stings me escuece
stockings las medias
stomach el estómago
stomach-ache un dolor de
  estómago
stop *(verb)* parar
  (bus stop etc) la parada
  stop! ¡alto!
storm la tormenta
strawberries las fresas
stream *(small river)* el arroyo
string la cuerda
student el estudiante

stupid estúpido
suburbs las afueras
sugar el azúcar
suit *(noun)* el traje
  (verb) sentar bien
  it suits you te sienta bien
suitcase la maleta
sun el sol
sunbathe tomar el sol
sunburn una quemadura de sol
sunglasses las gafas de sol
sunny soleado
  it's sunny hace sol
suntan el bronceado
suntan lotion la loción
  bronceadora
supermarket el supermercado
supplement el suplemento
sweat *(verb)* sudar
  (noun) el sudor
sweatshirt la camisa de deporte
sweet *(not sour)* dulce
  (candy) un caramelo
swimming costume el traje de
  baño
swimming pool la piscina
swimming trunks el bañador
Swiss suizo
switch el interruptor
Switzerland Suiza
synagogue la sinagoga

T-shirt la camiseta
table la mesa
tablet la pastilla
take tomar
take off *(noun)* el despegue
  (verb) despegar
talcum powder los polvos de
  talco

talk *(verb)* hablar
　(noun) una charla
tall alto
tampon el tamón
tangerine la mandarina
tap el grifo
tapestry el tapiz
tea el té
tea towel el paño de cocina
telegram el telegrama
telephone *(noun)* el teléfono
　(verb) telefonear
telephone box la cabina
　telefónica
telephone call la llamada
　telefónica
television la televisión
temperature *(heat)* la
　temperatura
　(fever) la fiebre
tent la tienda (de campaña)
tent peg la clavija (de la tienda)
tent pole el mástil
than que
thank *(verb)* agradecer
　thanks gracias
　thank you gracias
that: that man/woman ese
　hombre/esa mujer
　what's that? ¿qué es eso?
　I think that... creo que...
their su
　it's theirs es suyo
them: it's them son ellos
　it's for them es para ellos
　give it to them déselo
then entonces
there allí
thermos flask el termo
these: these things estas cosas
　these are mine éstos son míos
they ellos

thick grueso
thin delgado
think pensar
　I think so creo que sí
　I'll think about it lo pensaré
thirsty: I'm thirsty tengo sed
this: this man/woman este
　hombre/esta mujer
　what's this? ¿qué es esto?
　this is Mr... éste es el señor...
those: those things esas cosas
　those are his esos son suyos
throat la garganta
throat pastilles las pastillas para
　la garganta
through por
thunderstorm la tormenta
ticket *(train etc)* el billete
　(theatre etc) la entrada
tide la marea
tie *(noun)* la corbata
　(verb) atar
time tiempo
　what's the time? ¿qué hora
　es?
timetable el horario
tin una lata
　(material) hojalata
tin opener un abrelatas
tip *(money)* la propina
　(end) la punta
tired cansado
tissues los kleenex ®
to: to England a Inglaterra
　to the station a la estación
toast la tostada
tobacco el tabaco
today hoy
together juntos
toilet el wáter
toilet paper el papel higiénico
tomato el tomate

tomorrow mañana
tongue la lengua
tonic la tónica
tonight esta noche
too *(also)* también
  (excessive) demasiado
tooth el diente
  (back) la muela
toothache un dolor de muelas
toothbrush el cepillo de dientes
toothpaste la pasta dentífrica
torch la linterna
tour un viaje
tourist el turista
towel la toalla
tower la torre
town la ciudad
town hall el ayuntamiento
toy el juguete
toy shop la juguetería
track suit el chandal
tractor el tractor
tradition la tradición
traffic el tráfico
traffic lights el semáforo
trailer el remolque
train el tren
translate traducir
transmission la transmisión
travel agency la agencia de
  viajes
traveller's cheque un cheque
  de viajes
tray la bandeja
tree el arbol
trousers los pantalones
try intentar
tunnel el túnel
tweezers las pinzas
typewriter la máquina de
  escribir
tyre el neumático

umbrella el paraguas
uncle el tío
under debajo de
underground el metro
underpants los calzoncillos
university la universidad
unmarried soltero
until hasta
  until we get there hasta que
  lleguemos
unusual poco común
up arriba
  (upwards) hacia arriba
  to get up levantarse
urgent urgente
us: it's us somos nostros
  it's for us es para nosotros
  give it to us dénoslo
use *(noun)* el uso
  (verb) usar
  it's no use no sirve de nada
useful útil
usual corriente
usually en general

vacancies *(accommodation)*
  habitaciones libres
vacuum cleaner la aspiradora
vacuum flask el termo
valley el valle
valve la válvula
vanilla la vainilla
vase el jarrón
veal la (carne de) ternera
vegetables la verdura
vegetarian vegetariano
vehicle el vehículo

very muy
vest la camiseta
view la vista
viewfinder el visor de imagen
villa el chalet
village el pueblo
vinegar el vinagre
violin el violín
visa el visado
visit *(noun)* la visita
  (verb) visitar
visitor el visitante
  (tourist) el turista
vitamin tablets las vitaminas
vodka el vodka
voice la voz

wait esperar
waiter el camarero
waiting room la sala de espera
waitress la camarera
Wales Gales
walk *(verb)* andar
  (noun) el paseo
  to go for a walk ir de paseo
walkman ® el walkie-talkie
wall la pared
  (garden etc) la valla
wallet la cartera
war la guerra
wardrobe el armario
warm caliente
  (weather) caluroso
  it's warm hace calor
was: I was here (yo) estaba aquí
  he/she/it was in the room
  (el)/(ella) estaba en la
  habitación
washing powder el detergente
washing-up liquid el lavavajillas

wasp la avispa
watch *(noun)* el reloj
  (verb) mirar
water el agua
waterfall la cascada
wave *(noun: sea)* la ola
  (verb) agitar
  radio wave la onda de radio
we nosotros
weather el tiempo
wedding la boda
week la semana
wellingtons las botas de agua
Welsh galés
were: we were in London
  estábamos en Londres
  they were on holiday estaban
  de vacaciones
  where were you? ¿dónde
  estaba?
west el oeste
  west of the town al oeste de
  la ciudad
wet mojado
what? ¿qué?
wheel la rueda
wheelchair la silla de ruedas
when? ¿cuándo?
where? ¿dónde?
whether si
which ¿cuál?
whisky el whisky
wide ancho
  (big) grande
  3 metres wide de tres metros
  de anchura
wife la mujer
wind el viento
window la ventana
windscreen el parabrisas
windscreen wiper el
  limpiaparabrisas

wine el vino
  (red/white wine) vino
  tinto/blanco
wine list la carta de vinos
wine merchant el vinatero
wing el ala
with con
without sin
woman la mujer
wood *(forest)* el bosque
  (material) la madera
wool la lana
word la palabra
work *(noun)* el trabajo
  (verb) trabajar
worse peor
wrapping paper el papel de
  envolver
  (for presents) el papel de regalo
wrist la muñeca
writing paper el papel de
  escribir
wrong equivocado
  he took the wrong turning

se equivocó de camino

year el año
yellow amarillo
yes sí
yesterday ayer
yet: is it ready yet? ¿está listo
  ya?
  not yet todavía no
yoghurt el yogur
you *(singular familiar)* tú
  (plural familar) vosotros
  (polite singular) usted
  (polite plural) ustedes
your *(familiar singular)* tú
  (familiar plural) vuestro
  (singular polite) su
  (plural polite) su
  it's yours es tuyo/vuestro
youth hostel el albergue juvenil
zip la cremallera
zoo el zoo